All Color Book of
VEGETABLE DISHES

ARCO PUBLISHING INC.
New York

CONTENTS

Series editor: Mary Lambert

Published 1984 by
Arco Publishing, Inc.
215 Park Avenue South
New York, NY 10003

© Marshall Cavendish Books Limited 1984

**Library of Congress
Catalog Card Number: 84-70831**
ISBN 0-668-06217-7 cloth
ISBN 0-668-06223-1 paper

Printed in Italy

SYMBOLS

⏰	**TIME** 1-2 hours	!	**WATCHPOINT** Pitfalls that may occur during preparation
⏰	**TIME** Over 2 hours		
⚡	**SUPERQUICK** Under 1 hour to prepare and cook	✳	**FREEZING** When to freeze a dish
⏰	**TIME TRAP** Allow extra time for this recipe	🐾	**ECONOMY** Inexpensively made dishes

INTRODUCTION

Vegetables are so versatile, they can add goodness and color as accompaniments to a normal meal with meat or they can be made into tasty and nutritious main courses in their own right. *Vegetable dishes* contains nearly 80 easy-to-make recipes and has a varied mixture of appetizers, soups, salads, main dishes and accompanying dishes plus some more spicy vegetable dishes like *Cauliflower creole* or *Vegetable biriani* to add more interest to a special meal.

This book is ideal for vegetarians who want to try more exciting recipes or people who just love the taste and texture of vegetables and salads.

All the recipes have full color pictures to inspire the cook and they all contain cook's notes which give serving and buying ideas. The notes also tell you how much time the dish takes, how many calories it contains, and gives alternative fillings to make the dish more economic or perhaps more exotic.

APPETIZERS

Spring rolls

MAKES 6

10 oz beansprouts
8 scallions, cut into matchstick
    strips
1 red pepper, seeded, quartered and
    thinly sliced
1 cup thinly sliced
    mushrooms
3 tablespoons vegetable oil
1 slice fresh ginger root,
    finely chopped
1 tablespoon soy sauce
1 tablespoon dry sherry
freshly ground black pepper
vegetable oil, for deep frying
scallion tassels, to garnish

PASTRY

2 cups all-purpose flour
½ teaspoon salt
½ cup warm water

1 Make the pastry: Sift the flour and salt into a bowl, then make a well in the center and pour in the water. Mix with a wooden spoon until well blended, then knead well until the dough is soft and pliable. Wrap in plastic wrap and put in the refrigerator 30 minutes to chill.
2 Heat the oil in a large skillet or wok and add the beansprouts, the scallions and red pepper, mushrooms and ginger. Cook briskly, stirring, for 2 minutes, then add the soy sauce, sherry, and pepper to taste. Cook 1 further minute and remove from the heat.
3 Roll out the pastry on a lightly floured surface as thinly as possible to a neat rectangle, about 18 × 12 inches. Cut the pastry into six 6 inch squares.
4 Place 2 tablespoons of the vegetable mixture in the center of each pastry square. Fold in the sides, brush with a little water then carefully roll up. Dampen underside of pastry ends and press to seal.

5 Heat the oil in a deep-fat frier to 375° or until a stale bread cube browns in 50 seconds.
6 Using a slotted spoon lower 3 rolls into the oil and fry for about 5 minutes until crisp and golden. Remove with a slotted spoon and drain. Keep all the spring rolls warm while cooking the remainder (see Cook's tip).

Cook's Notes

TIME
1 hour to prepare, including chilling time, then 10 minutes cooking.

COOK'S TIP
The rolls may be made a few hours in advance, allowed to cool, then reheated in a 325° oven just before serving.

● 230 calories per roll

Egg and lettuce rolls

MAKES ABOUT 20

5 large crisp lettuce leaves (see Buying guide)
3 hard-cooked eggs, roughly chopped
2 tablespoons butter or margarine softened
¼ cup crumbled Danish Blue cheese

1 Cut off a thin slice from the stalk end of each lettuce leaf to remove the thickest part of the stalk. Wash and gently pat dry on paper towels. Set aside.
2 Make the filling: Put the eggs into a bowl with the butter and the cheese. Mash with a fork to form a smooth paste, adding a little more butter if the mixture is too stiff to blend.
3 Place 1 lettuce leaf on a work surface and spoon 1 tablespoon of the egg mixture into the center. Gently spread the mixture over the lettuce leaf right up to the edges. Starting at the trimmed end, tightly roll up the leaf to enclose the egg mixture. Wrap firmly in plastic wrap immediately after rolling.
4 Spread, roll and wrap the remaining lettuce leaves in the same way and refrigerate overnight.
5 To serve: Unwrap the rolls and cut with a sharp knife into 1-inch lengths. Serve at once.

Cook's Notes

 TIME
About 20 minutes preparation, plus overnight chilling.

 BUYING GUIDE
Choose a romaine or iceberg lettuce for this recipe.

 VARIATIONS
For a milder flavor, use a cream cheese instead of blue cheese and season with salt and pepper and a little paprika.
Alternatively, replace the blue cheese with anchovy paste, available in tubes and jars from delicatessens and specialty food stores.

 SERVING IDEAS
Serve as a summery appetizer, garnished with tomatoe wedges and cucumber slices. these rolls also make delicate accompaniments for cocktails — arrange attractively on a serving platter and garnish with tomato or sprigs of watercress and parsley for a pretty effect.

● 25 calories per roll

Spinach surprise

 SERVES 4

1 lb fresh spinach or ½ lb frozen chopped spinach
salt
¼ cup butter or margarine
1 onion, finely chopped
¼ cup all-purpose flour
⅔ cup milk
good pinch of freshly ground nutmeg
freshly ground black pepper
4 eggs, separated
1 tablespoon grated Parmesan cheese
butter, for greasing

1 If using fresh spinach, wash very thoroughly and remove the stems and central midribs. Place the spinach in a saucepan with only the water that clings to the leaves, and sprinkle with salt. Cover and cook over moderate heat for about 10 minutes, until the spinach is cooked, stirring occasionally. If using frozen spinach, cook according to package directions.

2 Drain the spinach well in a strainer, pressing out all the excess water. Chop the spinach, if using fresh. Grease a 1½ quart soufflé dish.

Preheat oven to 375°.

3 Melt the butter in a large saucepan, add the onion and cook over low heat for about 5 minutes until soft and lightly colored. Sprinkle in the flour and stir over low heat for 1-2 minutes until straw-colored. Remove from the heat and gradually stir in the milk. Return to moderate, heat and simmer, stirring, until thick.

4 Stir in the chopped spinach and grated nutmeg and season well with salt and pepper. Simmer over gentle heat 2 minutes.

5 Remove from the heat. Beat the egg yolks and beat them into the spinach mixture.

6 Beat the egg whites until they are just standing in soft peaks then fold gently into the spinach mixture with a metal spoon. [!]

7 Pour the mixture into the greased soufflé dish and sprinkle the top evenly with the grated Parmesan cheese. Bake in oven about 30-40 minutes until risen and lightly browned on the top. It should be firm to the touch on the outside, and not wobbly if gently shaken, but still moist in the center. Serve at once straight from the dish.

Cook's Notes

TIME
Preparation takes about 30 minutes cooking 30-40 minutes.

 SERVING IDEAS
This spinach dish is very versatile: serve as a light lunch or supper or as an appetizer. Or try it as a vegetable accompaniment: it goes very well with veal dishes.

For individual soufflés, bake in four 1¼ cup greased custard cups for 20-30 minutes, or eight ½ cup greased custard cups for 15-20 minutes.

WATCHPOINT
Do not overbeat the egg whites. It is easier to fold in the whites if you first beat 1-2 tablespoons of beaten whites into the spinach mixture to slacken it. Carefully fold in the whites so as not to lose the trapped air.

VARIATION
For a more substantial main-course dish, add ½ cup finely chopped cooked ham or chicken.

● 250 calories per portion

Mushroom puffs and cheese sauce

SERVES 4

12 cup mushrooms (see Buying guide)
1 sheet (½ of 17 oz package) frozen puff pastry, thawed
1 tablespoon butter
½ teaspoon dried marjoram
freshly ground black pepper
1 egg, lightly beaten

CHEESE SAUCE
1 oz blue cheese
⅔ cup plain yogurt
2 scallions, finely sliced
salt and freshly ground black pepper

1 Trim the mushroom stems level with the caps, then chop the stems finely and reserve.

2 Roll out the pastry thinly on a lightly floured surface. Then, using a 3-inch fluted cookie cutter, cut out 24 pastry rounds.

3 Place one mushroom, stem side up, on each of 12 pastry circles. Put a small knob of butter, a pinch of marjoram and a sprinkling of pepper on each mushroom.

4 Brush the edges of each mushroom-topped pastry circle with beaten egg, then place a second circle of pastry on top. Bring together the pastry edges, pressing well to seal. Crimp the edges.

5 Dampen 2 cookie sheets and transfer the puffs to them. Cover the puffs with plastic wrap and refrigerate 15 minutes.

6 Preheat the oven to 425°.

7 Meanwhile, make the cheese sauce: Crumble the cheese into a serving bowl, add a little yogurt and mix together with a fork until fairly smooth. Stir in the remaining yogurt, reserved mushroom stems and half the scallions. Sprinkle the remaining scallions on top of the sauce, cover with plastic wrap and refrigerate.

8 Brush the tops of the puffs with the remaining beaten egg, then bake in the oven 10-15 minutes until well-risen and golden brown.

9 Pile the hot puffs onto a warm serving plate and serve with the chilled sauce handed separately (see Serving ideas).

Cook's Notes

TIME
Preparing the puffs takes 15-20 minutes. Allow 15 minutes chilling and 10-15 minutes baking. Making the sauce takes 5 minutes.

SERVING IDEAS
These mushroom puffs make an ideal appetizer to a meal. Allow 3 puffs per person and serve on plates garnished with celery or scallion tassels and, if liked, sliced raw mushrooms, and small lettuce leaves.

BUYING GUIDE
Cultivated cup mushrooms are larger than button mushrooms: their caps have begun to open. Choose mushrooms about 1¼ inches wide, so the caps will hold the butter and be the right size for the pastry rounds.

Buy a 17 oz package of ready-made frozen puff pastry and use 1 sheet for this recipe. Keep the remaining sheet frozen for another use.

● 340 calories per portion

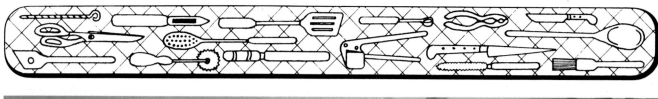

Grapefruit and celery salad

SERVES 4

2 large grapefruits
2 heads celery
4 teaspoons chopped fresh mint
2 tablespoons seedless raisins
4 sprigs mint, to garnish

DRESSING
⅔ cup plain yogurt, chilled
1 tablespoon olive oil
1 tablespoon orange juice
salt
freshly ground black pepper

1 Cut each grapefruit in half, into a waterlily shape (see Preparation). Scoop out the flesh, using a curved grapefruit knife. (Alternatively run a small sharp knife between the flesh and the peel, taking care not to pierce the peel, then remove the flesh). Reserve the shells in the refrigerator.

2 Discard the pith, membranes and pits and put the grapefruit flesh into a bowl.

3 Remove and discard the outer stalks of the celery, leaving the tender, yellowy "hearts" (see Economy). Cut the celery hearts into ¼-inch slices.

4 Add the sliced celery to the bowl, together with the chopped mint and raisins. Toss well.

5 Make the dressing: Stir together the yogurt, olive oil and orange juice and season to taste with salt and pepper.

6 Add the dressing to the salad, toss well and pile the salad into the grapefruit shells. Refrigerate the filled shells 30 minutes. Garnish the salad with mint sprigs and serve (see Cook's tip).

Cook's Notes

TIME
Preparation takes about 40 minutes.

COOK'S TIP
The shells may be stored and re-used in another dish: wash, pat dry and store for a few days covered in the refrigerator or wrap them and freeze.

ECONOMY
Reserve the outer stalks and leaves of the celery for stock or soup.

PREPARATION
To cut the grapefruits into waterlilies:

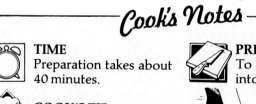

Insert knife at an angle through side into center. Make second cut to form v-shape. Continue all round the grapefruit and pull apart.

● 100 calories per portion

Vegetable samosas

MAKES 12

¾ lb potatoes, diced
½ lb package frozen mixed
    vegetables
1 tablespoon vegetable oil
1 onion, finely chopped
1 tablespoon curry powder
6 tablespoons water
salt and freshly ground black pepper
vegetable oil, for deep frying

PASTRY
1½ cups all-purpose flour
salt
2 tablespoons butter or margarine,
    diced
about 4 tablespoons water

1 Make the pastry: sift the flour and salt into a bowl. Add the butter and cut it into the flour slowly until the whole mixture resembles fine bread crumbs. Then mix in just enough water to make a soft elastic dough. Wrap dough in plastic wrap and refrigerate 30 minutes.

2 Meanwhile, make the filling: Heat the oil in a saucepan, add the onion and fry gently 5 minutes until soft and lightly colored.

3 Stir in the curry powder, then add the potatoes and cook further 1-2 minutes.

4 Add the mixed vegetables, water and salt and pepper to taste. Bring to a boil, stirring all the time Lower the heat slightly, cover and simmer for 15-20 minutes, stirring occasionally, until all the vegetables are tender. Allow to cool slightly.

5 Divide the dough into 12 pieces and roll out each piece on a floured surface to a 4-inch square.

6 Place 1 tablespoon filling in the center of each square. Brush the edges of the pastry with water and bring over one corner to form a triangle. Press the sides together and crimp. ✳

7 Heat the oil in a deep-fat frier with a basket to 350°, or until a day-old bread cube browns in 60 seconds. Put 3 samosas into the basket, then lower into the oil and cook 2 minutes or until the pastry bubbles and turns golden. Drain on paper towels and keep warm while cooking the remaining samosas in the same way. Serve at once.

Cook's Notes

TIME
Samosas take about 35 minutes preparation and cooking, plus 30 minutes chilling time.

FREEZING
Freeze the samosas before cooking: Open freeze until solid, then pack into a rigid container or polythene bag. Seal, label and return to the freezer for up to 3 months. To serve: Deep-fry from frozen for about 3-4 minutes.

SERVING IDEAS
Samosas are a favorite Indian snack. Serve them as an appetizer to an Indian meal with mango chutney, or with a tasty sauce made by blending plain yogurt with mint, finely chopped cucumber, salt and freshly ground black pepper to taste.

● 155 calories per samosa

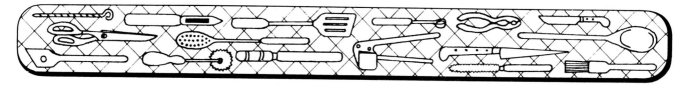

Stuffed green peppers

SERVES 4
4 green peppers (see Buying guide)
⅔ cup long-grain rice
1 small onion, chopped
3 tablespoons vegetable oil
2 tablespoons tomato paste
5 tablespoons water
½ cup slivered almonds
⅓ cup golden raisins
2 teaspoons dried oregano
grated rind of 1 orange
salt and freshly ground black pepper

1 Preheat oven to 350°.
2 Bring a large saucepan of water to the boil, add the rice, bring back to boil and cook about 15 minutes until the rice is tender.
3 Meanwhile, slice the tops off the peppers and reserve them. Carefully seed the peppers.
4 Drain the rice thoroughly, rinse under cold running water and then drain again.
5 In a bowl, thoroughly mix the rice together with all the remaining ingredients, reserving 2 tablespoons of oil and 2 tablespoons of the water.
6 Fill the peppers with the stuffing mixture, packing it in well but taking care not to break the peppers.
7 Put the peppers into a casserole in which they will stand together closely but comfortably (see Cook's tip). Replace the tops.

8 Mix together the reserved oil and water and drizzle it over the peppers.

9 Cover the dish and bake 25 minutes. Uncover and bake 25 minutes. Serve hot, warm or cold.

Cook's Notes

TIME
Preparation takes about 30 minutes, including cooking the rice. Cooking in the oven takes 50 minutes.

BUYING GUIDE
Buy firm, squat peppers as they stand up better in the dish and the stuffing will not fall out.

COOK'S TIP
If necessary, put a little crumpled foil between the peppers to keep them upright and remove it before serving.

VARIATION
Red peppers could be used instead of green or use 2 of each.

SERVING IDEAS
These make a filling first course on their own or with a tomato sauce, served with hot garlic or pita bread. They are especially good served warm. They could also be served as a tasty supper dish.

● 325 calories per portion

Vegetable kabobs

SERVES 4

3 small zucchini, cut into 1½-inch
    slices
12 whole baby white onions
salt
12 whole small mushrooms
8 tomatoes, halved
8 small bay leaves
¼ cup butter or margarine,
    melted
vegetable oil, for greasing

MARINADE
6 tablespoons vegetable oil
1 tablespoon lemon juice
1 small onion, finely chopped
2 tablespoons chopped fresh
    parsley
1 clove garlic, crushed (optional)
salt and freshly ground black pepper

1 Bring a saucepan of salted water
to a boil, add the zucchini slices
and white onions and boil gently for
1 minute. Drain and immediately
plunge the vegetables into cold
water to prevent them cooking
further. Drain vegetables well again
and pat dry with paper towels.
2 Divide the zucchini slices, onions,
mushrooms, tomatoes and bay
leaves into 4 equal
portions and

thread them onto 4 greased metal
kabob skewers, alternating the
shapes and colors as much as
possible. Lay the skewers in a
shallow dish.
3 To make the marinade: Put all the
ingredients in a screw-top jar with
salt and pepper to taste. Shake well
to mix. Pour the marinade over the
vegetable kabobs and leave them in
a cool place for about 2 hours,
turning them occasionally to coat
the vegetables evenly.
4 Preheat broiler to moderate. Lift
the kabobs from the marinade and
allow any excess dressing to drain

off. Brush the vegetables with the
melted butter. Broil the kabobs
about 8 minutes, turning them
frequently to brown the vegetables
evenly. Serve at once, while hot.

Cook's Notes

TIME
Preparation takes about
25 minutes, marinating
2 hours, cooking 8 minutes.

SERVING IDEAS
Serve on a bed of herb-
flavored rice.

● 230 calories per portion

Mixed vegetable croquettes

MAKES 16

2 onions, very finely chopped
6 celery stalks, very finely chopped
2 carrots, grated
1½ cups very finely chopped mushrooms
1 tablespoon vegetable oil
1 tablespoon smooth peanut butter
½ cup unsalted peanuts, ground or very finely chopped
1½ cups fresh whole wheat bread crumbs
pinch of dried mixed herbs
salt and freshly ground black pepper
2 eggs, beaten
¾ cup dried bread crumbs (see Economy)
vegetable oil, for deep-frying

1 Heat the oil in a large saucepan, add the onions and celery and cook gently 5 minutes. Do not allow the vegetables to brown.
2 Add the carrots and mushrooms to the pan and continue cooking a further 5 minutes, stirring from time to time.
3 Remove from the heat, then stir in the peanut butter until well combined. Add the peanuts, whole wheat bread crumbs, herbs and salt and pepper to taste. Mix well and bind with half the beaten eggs. Leave until cool enough to handle.
4 Meanwhile, pour the remaining beaten eggs into a shallow bowl or onto a plate. Place the dried bread crumbs on a separate plate, ready to coat the croquettes.
5 When the mixture is cool, divide it into 16 portions and shape them into croquettes. Dip each croquette in the beaten eggs, then roll in the bread crumbs until thoroughly coated.
6 Pour enough vegetable oil into a deep-fat frier to come to a depth of 1½ inches. Heat the oil to 350° or until a 1-inch stale bread cube browns in 60 seconds. Lower in the croquettes and deep-fry 3 minutes, or until golden brown (see Cook's tip). Drain the croquettes very thoroughly on paper towels and serve hot.

Cook's Notes

TIME
Preparation of the croquette mixture, cooling and shaping take about 40 minutes. Heating the oil and deep-frying take about 10 minutes.

ECONOMY
Dried bread crumbs are available commercially in packages and drums, but it is easy, and more economical, to make them at home. Save crusts or stale bread. Cut the bread into pieces and dry it out in a very cool oven or place in the oven as it cools down after cooking the main meal of the day: this method may require repeating 2 or 3 times. When the bread is dry and golden brown, crush it with a rolling pin or process in a blender. Store the crumbs in a screw-top jar.

VARIATIONS
Experiment with different coatings for the croquettes. Try flavoring the dried bread crumbs with a little curry powder or paprika, or use finely crushed cornflakes or potato chips (plain or flavored) as a tasty substitute for the dried breadcrumbs.

COOK'S TIP
If you do not have a deep-fat frier, you can shallow-fry the croquettes. Heat oil to a depth of about 1-inch in a large, deep skillet and cook the croquettes over moderate heat for 10 minutes until golden brown. Turn the croquettes over once during cooking so that the croquettes are evenly browned on both sides.

● 125 calories per croquette

Herby dip with cheese crackers

SERVES 4

1 cup grated mild cheese
½ cup sweet butter,
   softened
1 tablespoon chopped chives
1 tablespoon finely chopped fresh
   fennel leaves or mint
1 tablespoon finely chopped fresh
   parsley
¼ teaspoon paprika
¼ teaspoon caraway seeds
4 tablespoons milk
salt and freshly ground black
   pepper

CHEESE CRACKERS

½ cup butter, softened
1 cup grated sharp Cheddar
   cheese
1 cup whole wheat flour
2 tablespoons sesame seeds
butter, for greasing

Cook's Notes

TIME
30 minutes to prepare and cook the crackers 15 minutes to make the dip.

SERVING IDEAS
Serve as an unusual appetizer at a dinner party or, accompanied by a vege-table soup, as a quick supper dish. Alternatively, cut out the crackers with tiny petits fours cutters or cut into small straws and serve at a drinks party.

The crackers may be served while still slightly warm.

● 685 calories per portion

1 Make the crackers: Preheat oven to 400° and lightly grease a cookie sheet. Sift the flour.
2 In a large bowl, beat the butter until pale and creamy, then beat in the cheese. Add the flour a little at a time, beating thoroughly after each addition, to form a stiff dough.
3 Sprinkle the sesame seeds on a lightly floured work surface and roll out the dough, until it is about ⅛-inch thick. Cut the dough into about 12 rounds using a lightly floured 3-inch cookie cutter.
4 Using a spatula, transfer the rounds to the prepared cookie sheet, spacing them apart, then bake 5-8 minutes until golden.
5 Remove from the oven, allow to settle 1-2 minutes, then transfer to a wire rack and allow to cool.
6 Meanwhile, make the dip: Put the grated mild cheese into a bowl with the butter, herbs, paprika, caraway seeds and milk. Beat until blended and creamy, then season to taste with salt and pepper.
7 Spoon the mixture into a small serving dish, smooth over the surface and serve with the crackers.

Spicy bean pâté

SERVES 4

1 can (about 1 lb) red kidney beans
1 clove garlic, crushed (optional)
1 tablespoon tomato paste
1 teaspoon Worcestershire sauce
1 teaspoon lemon juice
few drops of hot-pepper sauce
salt and freshly ground black pepper
parsley sprigs, to garnish

1 Drain the beans, reserving the liquid from the can.
2 Put all the ingredients into a blender and blend to a smooth paste; it will be flecked with pieces of bean skin. Alternatively, place all the ingredients in a bowl, pound them with the end of a rolling pin, then mash thoroughly with a fork. If the mixture becomes too thick, add 2-3 tablespoons of the reserved liquid from the can.
3 Taste and adjust seasoning.

4 Pack the pâté into 4 small custard cups or individual dishes and carefully smooth the surface of each with a small knife. Serve the pâté cold or chilled, garnished with parsley sprigs.

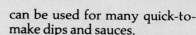

Cook's Notes

TIME
Preparation of this pâté takes 15 minutes.

COOK'S TIP
The pâté may be prepared up to 2 days before then stored in the refrigerator.

BUYING GUIDE
Different canned pulses can be a very handy pantry shelf standby. They can be used for many quick-to-make dips and sauces.

SERVING IDEAS
Serve as a quick, easy and different appetizer with brown bread or toast. For a party, serve the pâté as a dip with sticks of carrot, celery stalks and sliced cucumber, or spread it on cocktail crackers.

●65 calories per portion

Avocado dip

SERVES 4-6

2 ripe avocados (see Buying guide)
juice of 1 lemon
1 clove garlic, crushed (optional)
4 tomatoes, skinned, seeded and
    finely chopped
1 small onion, finely chopped
4 tablespoons finely chopped celery
2–3 tablespoons olive oil
1 tablespoon chopped fresh parsley
salt and freshly ground black pepper

1 Cut the avocados in half length-wise (see Cook's tip), remove the seeds then scoop out the flesh with a teaspoon. Put the flesh in a bowl and mash it with a wooden spoon.

2 Add the lemon juice, garlic, if using, tomatoes, onion and celery.

3 Stir in enough olive oil to make a soft, smooth mixture, then add the chopped parsley and season with salt and pepper to taste.

4 Transfer the dip to a serving bowl, cover with plastic wrap and chill in the refrigerator about 30 minutes. Serve chilled.

Cook's Notes

 TIME
This dip takes 20 minutes preparation, then 30 minutes chilling.

BUYING GUIDE
Avocados are ripe when the flesh at the rounded end yields slightly when gently pressed. Reject any avocados that are hard or very soft or have blotched, dry skins.

COOK'S TIPS
When cutting the avocado, use a stainless steel knife to prevent the avocado flesh from coloring at the beginning.

 SERVING IDEAS
Serve with a selection of small crackers, potato chips or crisp raw vegetables.

● 325 calories per portion

Lima bean dip with crudités

SERVES 8

½ cup dried lima beans,
    soaked in cold water overnight
    (see Cook's tips)
4-6 tablespoons good-quality olive
    oil
1 tablespoon red wine vinegar
1 clove garlic, crushed (optional)
salt and freshly ground black pepper

CRUDITES
1 small cauliflower, broken into
    flowerets
1 cucumber, cut into sticks
2 celery stalks, cut into sticks
2 carrots, cut into sticks
1 small green pepper, seeded and cut
    into strips
1 small red pepper, seeded and cut
    into strips
bunch of radishes

1 Drain the beans and rinse thoroughly under cold running water. Put them in a large saucepan, cover with fresh cold water and bring to a boil. Lower the heat, half cover with a lid and simmer about 1¼ hours or until the beans are tender. Add more water to the pan during the cooking time if necessary.

2 Drain the beans, reserving the cooking liquid. Put the beans in a blender with 4 tablespoons oil, the vinegar, garlic, if using, a little salt and pepper and 4 tablespoons of the reserved cooking liquid. Blend until thick and smooth, adding a little more liquid if the mixture is too thick.

3 Taste and adjust seasoning, then spoon the mixture into a small bowl and fork over the top; or heap the mixture up in the center of a large flat serving plate.

4 Serve the crudités in a shallow basket or salad bowl, or stand the bowl of dip in the center of a large plate and arrange the crudités around the edge of the plate. If you like, drizzle 2 tablespoons oil over the top of the dip just before serving (see Did you know). Serve at room temperature or refrigerate about 1 hour before serving and serve the dip chilled.

Cook's Notes

TIME
Cooking the dried beans takes 1¼ hours and preparing the dip then takes 30 minutes.

COOK'S TIPS
If you do not have time to soak the beans in cold water overnight, you can cut down the soaking time considerably by using hot water. Put the beans in a large saucepan, cover with cold water and bring to the boil. Drain and repeat, then remove from the heat and leave to soak in the hot water 2 hours.

To save even more time, you could use 1 can (about 1 lb) cannellini beans, which are precooked. The whole dip can then be made within 30 minutes.

PRESSURE COOKING
Dried lima beans can be cooked in a pressure cooker. Soak and rinse as in recipe, then cook at high (H) pressure 20 minutes.

SERVING IDEAS
The lima bean dip makes an appetizer for 8 or a filling salad meal for 4.

FREEZING
The dip freezes well, either in the dish from which it will be served or in a rigid container. Store for up to 3 months and allow 2 hours thawing at room temperature before serving.

DID YOU KNOW
Finishing off the dip with extra oil drizzled on top is usual in Middle Eastern countries, where dips and pâtés made from pulses are very popular. If you do not like too oily a taste, this can be easily omitted.

● 225 calories per portion

SOUPS

Brussels soup

SERVES 4

1 lb Brussels sprouts
1 tablespoon vegetable oil
1 small onion, chopped
2 tablespoons medium sherry
    (optional)
3 cups chicken broth
freshly grated nutmeg
salt and ground black pepper

1 Heat the oil in a saucepan, add the onion and fry gently for 5 minutes until soft and lightly colored.
2 Stir in the sherry, if using, then add the broth. Bring to a boil, add the sprouts, a pinch of nutmeg and salt and pepper to taste. Lower the heat slightly, cover and simmer about 30 minutes.
3 Pass the soup through a strainer, or leave to cool slightly, then purée in a blender. ✴ Return the soup to the rinsed pan and heat through.
4 Taste and adjust seasoning, then pour immediately into warmed individual soup bowls. Sprinkle each serving with a pinch of nutmeg and serve (see Special occasion).

Cook's Notes

TIME
Preparation and cooking only take about 40 minutes.

SPECIAL OCCASION
Swirl a little light cream into the soup immediately before serving. Alternatively, serve with fried bread croutons or crumbled crisply fried fatty bacon.

FREEZING
Cool the soup and pour into a rigid container. Seal, label and freeze for up to 4 months. To serve: Reheat from frozen in a heavy-based pan, stirring frequently to prevent sticking. Taste and adjust seasoning before pouring into warmed soup bowls.

●75 calories per portion

Cream of chestnut soup

SERVES 4-6

1½ lb fresh chestnuts
5 cups chicken broth
1 bay leaf
2 onions, sliced
about ⅔ cup milk
1 egg yolk
⅔ cup heavy cream
pinch of freshly grated nutmeg
salt and freshly ground black pepper
1-2 teaspoons sugar

1 Nick the chestnuts with a sharp knife, then place in a saucepan and cover with cold water. Gradually bring to a boil and simmer 10 minutes.

2 Remove the pan from the heat, then take out the chestnuts, a few at a time (see Cook's tip). Remove both the outside and inside skins.

3 Put the peeled chestnuts into a large pan together with the chicken broth, bay leaf and onions. Bring to a boil, then lower the heat, cover and simmer gently 1½ hours.

4 Remove the bay leaf, then press the soup through a strainer or work in a blender.

5 Return the soup to the rinsed-out pan and gradually stir in enough milk to make it a smooth con-sistency. Heat through gently. Blend the egg yolk and cream in a bowl. Remove the pan from the heat and stir in the egg and cream. Reheat but do not boil. [!]

6 Add the nutmeg, and season to taste with salt and pepper. Add the sugar, a little at a time, to taste. Pour into warmed individual soup bowls and serve at once.

Cook's Notes

TIME
Preparation takes 45-60 minutes (peeling the chestnuts is a lengthy process). Cooking 1½ hours, blending and finishing the soup, 15 minutes.

SERVING IDEAS
This is a substantial soup, ideal to serve on cold days with chunky slices of bread and butter and wedges of cheese.

COOK'S TIP
Keeping the chestnuts in hot water makes them easier to peel. If they are drained the skins toughen.

WATCHPOINT
Take care not to boil the soup at this stage as the egg and cream may overheat and curdle, and spoil the appearance of the dish.

● 460 calories per portion

Lentil and lemon soup

SERVES 4

½ cup split red lentils
1 tablespoon butter or margarine
2 celery stalks, chopped
1 medium onion, finely chopped
1 quart boiling water
2 chicken bouillon cubes
grated rind and juice of 1 lemon
¼ teaspoon ground cumin
　(optional)
salt and freshly ground black pepper
1 red pepper, seeded and thinly
　sliced into rings

TO GARNISH
1 lemon, thinly sliced
chopped chives (optional)

1 Melt the butter in a saucepan, add the celery and onion, then cover and cook gently 4 minutes.
2 Remove the pan from the heat, then stir in the lentils and water, with bouillon cubes. Add the lemon rind and juice, and the cumin, if using. Season to taste with salt and pepper. Cover and simmer over very gentle heat 30 minutes.
3 Add the sliced pepper to the pan, cover and cook a further 30 minutes. Taste and adjust seasoning. ✳
4 Pour the soup into warmed serving bowls, float the lemon slices on top, then sprinkle over the chives, if using. Serve at once.

Cook's Notes

TIME
Preparation 20 minutes; cooking takes 65 minutes.

FREEZING
Cool quickly, then freeze without the lemon and chives in a rigid polythene container or freezer bag (do not use foil containers, or the acid in the soup may react against the foil). Seal, label and freeze for up to 6 months. Thaw at room temperature, then reheat until bubbling, adding a little more water if necessary.

SERVING IDEAS
Warm crusty rolls are ideal to serve with this soup. For a luxurious touch, top each serving with 1 tablespoon dairy sour cream.

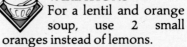
VARIATIONS
For a lentil and orange soup, use 2 small oranges instead of lemons.
　If chives are unavailable, use chopped scallion tops or parsley, if using another garnish as well as the lemon.

● 135 calories per portion

Cream of potato soup

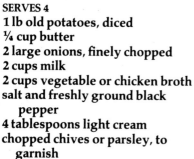

SERVES 4

1 lb old potatoes, diced
¼ cup butter
2 large onions, finely chopped
2 cups milk
2 cups vegetable or chicken broth
salt and freshly ground black
    pepper
4 tablespoons light cream
chopped chives or parsley, to
    garnish

1 Melt the butter in a large pan and, when the foam has subsided, add the potatoes and onions and cook gently about 5 minutes until the vegetables are soft. Stir frequently to prevent any of the potato dice or chopped onion from sticking to the bottom of the pan.
2 Add the milk and broth (see Cook's tip), season to taste with salt and pepper and bring to a boil. Lower heat and simmer 30 minutes, stirring occasionally, until the potatoes are tender.
3 Allow the mixture to cool a little, then work through a strainer or purée in an electric blender.
4 Return the soup to the rinsed-out pan and reheat. Taste and adjust the seasoning, if necessary, and stir in cream just before serving. [!] Pour into a large tureen, or ladle into individual soup bowls, garnish with the chopped chives or parsley and serve at once (see Serving ideas).

 TIME
Preparing and cooking take about 1 hour.

COOK'S TIP
The flavor of this soup is vastly improved by the use of homemade broth, rather than a bouillon cube.

SERVING IDEA
This filling soup makes a delicious lunch or supper dish served with slices of hot bread.

 VARIATIONS
Instead of using herbs as a garnish, sprinkle the cream of potato soup with paprika or a chopped hard-cooked egg.

WATCHPOINT
Once the cream has been added to the soup, do not allow it to boil, otherwise the cream will separate and spoil the appearance of the soup.

● 305 calories per portion

Green bean soup

SERVES 4

1 lb frozen cut green beans
   (see Buying guide)
3 cups chicken broth
1 small onion, chopped
bay leaf
parsley sprig
about ½ teaspoon Worcestershire
   sauce
salt and freshly ground black pepper

BEURRE MANIE (kneaded butter)
1 tablespoon all-purpose flour
1 tablespoon butter

TO GARNISH
6 black olives, pitted and finely
   chopped
1 hard-cooked egg, finely chopped

1 Pour the broth into a pan, bring to a boil and add the beans, onion, bay leaf and parsley. Bring back to a boil, then lower the heat, cover and simmer about 15 minutes until the beans are soft.

2 Discard the bay leaf and parsley. Allow the soup to cool slightly, then work in a blender until smooth. Return to the rinsed-out pan and set over low heat.

3 Make the beurre manié: Blend the flour and butter together with a spatula to make a paste, then cut the paste into pea-sized pieces. Beat the pieces into the soup and bring to the boil. Add Worcestershire sauce and salt and pepper to taste. Simmer for a further minute, then remove from heat.

4 Pour the soup into a warmed tureen or 4 individual soup bowls. Mix together the olives and egg, sprinkle over the soup and serve at once (see Serving ideas).

Cook's Notes

TIME
This soup takes about 30 minutes to prepare.

SERVING GUIDE
Serve hot with Melba toast or chill and garnish just before serving.

BUYING GUIDE
Fresh green beans can be used, but you will need about 1¼ lb to allow for trimming ends and side strings. Cut into pieces and cook as described. If the fresh beans are not particularly young and small, blanch them in boiling water 2 minutes to remove any bitterness before starting.

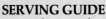

● 90 calories per portion

Chunky soy vegetable soup

SERVES 4

- ½ cup soybeans, soaked in cold water overnight (see Watchpoint)
- 1 tablespoon vegetable oil
- 1 large onion, sliced
- 2 leeks, thickly sliced
- 1 carrot, thickly sliced
- 2 celery stalks, thickly sliced
- 1 small turnip, cubed
- 3 cups chicken broth
- 1 tablespoon lemon juice
- 2 tablespoons tomato paste
- 1-2 teaspoons dried mixed herbs
- ¼ lb zucchini, thickly sliced
- a few tender cabbage or spinach leaves, finely shredded or chopped
- salt and freshly ground black pepper
- 2 teaspoons toasted sesame seeds, to garnish (optional)

1 Drain the soaked beans, then put into a saucepan and cover with fresh cold water. Bring to a boil and boil 10 minutes, then lower heat, cover and carefully simmer about 1½ hours.

2 After the beans have been cooking 1 hour 20 minutes, heat the oil in a separate large saucepan. Add the sliced onion and cook very gently 2-3 minutes until brown. Add the leeks, carrots, celery and turnips and cook, stirring, a further 2 minutes.

3 Stir in the chicken broth, lemon juice, tomato paste and the dried mixed herbs.

4 Drain the beans and add to the pan. Bring to a boil, then lower the heat slightly, cover the pan and then keep simmering gently for about 1 hour.

5 Add the zucchini and cabbage and continue to cook a further 15 minutes or until the vegetables and beans are tender. Season to taste with salt and pepper.

6 Pour into warmed individual soup bowls and garnish with a sprinkling of sesame seeds, if liked. Serve the soup at once.

Cook's Notes

TIME
Soaking the beans over-night, then 15 minutes preparation and 2¾ hours cooking time including pre-cooking the beans.

VARIATIONS
Add 1 can (about 8 oz) of peeled tomatoes in-stead of the tomato paste.

DID YOU KNOW
Soybeans look quite round in their dried form, but revert to an oval shape after soaking. They are very high in protein, making them an economical meat substitute.

ECONOMY
If possible, buy turnips with their green tops and used the tops in the soup instead of the cabbage leaves.

WATCHPOINT
Do not soak the soy-beans for longer than 12 hours and always stand the bowl in a cool place.

SERVING IDEAS
Serve with small bowls of grated cheese and fried bread croutons to sprinkle over the soup.

● 220 calories per portion

Jerusalem artichoke soup

SERVES 4-6

 2 lb Jerusalem artichokes (see Preparation)

 1 tablespoon butter or margarine
2 onions, chopped
2½ cups milk
2 cups chicken broth
salt and freshly ground black pepper
chopped fresh parsley

1 Melt the butter in a large saucepan, add the onions and cook gently for 5 minutes until soft and lightly colored.
2 Add the artichokes to the pan, together with the milk, broth and salt and pepper to taste.
3 Bring to a boil, reduce the heat slightly, cover and simmer about 30 minutes, until the artichokes are soft.
4 Leave to cool slightly, then work in a blender or food processor until smooth. Or work through a vegetable mill.

5 Return the soup to the rinsed-out pan and reheat gently. Taste and adjust seasoning, then pour into warmed individual soup bowls. Serve at once, garnished with chopped parsley.

Sunshine soup

SERVES 4

**2 lb pumpkin, seeded and
cut into 1-inch cubes
(see Variation)**
 salt
3 tablespoons butter
1 large onion, finely chopped
2 tomatoes, peeled and chopped
1 teaspoon chopped chives
¼ teaspoon freshly grated nutmeg
1 tablespoon shredded coconut
2½ cups chicken broth
freshly ground black pepper
1¼ cups light cream
paprika, to garnish

1 Put the pumpkin into a saucepan, add enough water just to cover and a good pinch of salt. Bring to a boil, then lower the heat slightly and simmer 15 minutes. Drain well.

2 Melt the butter in a saucepan, add the onion and cook gently 5 minutes until soft and lightly colored.
3 Add the pumpkin, tomatoes, chives, nutmeg and coconut and cook gently a further 5 minutes.
4 Pour in the broth, season with salt and pepper to taste and bring to a boil. Lower the heat slightly, cover and simmer about 30 minutes.
5 Remove the pan from the heat, allow to cool slightly, then purée in a blender. ✳ Then stir in half of the cream.
6 Pour the soup into warmed soup bowls, then swirl in the remaining cream and sprinkle with paprika. Serve at once.

Cook's Notes

TIME
10 minutes preparation, 55 minutes cooking including simmering pumpkin.

FREEZING
Pour the purée into a rigid container, leaving headspace. Cool quickly, then seal, label and freeze for up to 3 months. To serve: Thaw at room temperature for about 4 hours, then heat through and add the cream and paprika.

VARIATION
If you are unable to buy pumpkin, carrots are a very good substitute and they do not need precooking.

SERVING IDEAS
This soup is good either hot or cold. Serve with crusty whole wheat bread and chunks of Cheddar cheese for a light supper.

● 185 calories per portion

Carrot soup with egg and rice

SERVES 4-8

1½ lb new carrots, thinly sliced
2 tablespoons butter or margarine
2½ cups chicken broth
1 teaspoon sugar
salt and freshly ground black
   pepper
⅔ cup milk
½ cup cooked rice (see
   Cook's tips)
4 eggs at room temperature (see
   Cook's tips)
2 scallions, finely chopped
⅔ cup light cream

1 Melt the butter in a saucepan, add the carrots and cook gently 2-3 minutes to soften slightly.
2 Add the chicken broth and sugar and season to taste with salt and pepper. Bring to a boil, then lower the heat and simmer, uncovered, 30 minutes or until the carrots are very tender.
3 Remove the pan from the heat and allow mixture to cool slightly, then pour it into the goblet of a blender and work for a few seconds until smooth. Return the purée to the rinsed-out pan and stir in the milk and cooked rice. Taste and adjust the seasoning, if necessary.
4 Heat the soup gently until hot but not boiling, then break in the eggs and poach them for about 8 minutes or until they are firm enough to be lifted out with a slotted spoon.
5 Spoon an egg into each of 4 warmed soup bowls and pour over the soup. Sprinkle over the scallions, swirl in the cream and serve the soup at once.

Creamy mushroom soup

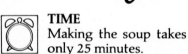

SERVES 4

½ lb small mushrooms (see Buying guide)
¼ cup butter
2 tablespoons all-purpose flour
2½ cups milk
⅓ cup cream cheese with chives
2 teaspoons lemon juice
salt and freshly ground black pepper
1 tablespoon chopped chives, to garnish

Cook's Notes

TIME
Making the soup takes only 25 minutes.

BUYING GUIDE
Choose small-sized or cup mushrooms for this recipe. Their delicate flavor blends well with the soft cheese. There is no need to pare them before using.

The larger open mushrooms may be used but the flavor will be stronger and the color slightly darker.

VARIATION
This is a thick creamy soup; if you prefer a thinner soup use only 1 tablespoon flour and replace 1¼ cups milk with a well-flavored chicken broth.

WATCHPOINT
Take care not to boil the soup after adding the cheese and mushrooms or it may spoil the flavor.

● 270 calories per serving

1 Finely chop the mushrooms, reserving 2-3 whole ones for the garnish. Melt half the butter in a skillet. Add the chopped mushrooms and cook gently about 5 minutes until soft. Set aside.
2 Melt the remaining butter in a large saucepan, sprinkle in flour and stir over low heat 1-2 minutes until it is straw-colored. Remove from the heat and gradually stir in milk. Return to the heat and simmer, stirring, until the mixture is thick and smooth.
3 Remove from the heat, add the cheese a little at a time and stir until melted. Stir in the mushrooms, their juices and the lemon juice. Season to taste. Return to heat and simmer 2-3 minutes. [!]
4 Pour into 4 warmed soup bowls. Float a few slices of mushrooms on top of each serving. Sprinkle lightly with chives and serve at once.

Chilled pea and bean soup

SERVES 4

1½ lb peas, shelled, and 6 of the best pods reserved (see Cook's tip)
1 lb lima beans, shelled
2 tablespoons butter or margarine
1 large onion, finely chopped
4 cups chicken broth
1 sprig fresh mint
salt and freshly ground black pepper
⅔ cup plain yogurt
¼ teaspoon curry paste
1 clove garlic, crushed (optional)
4 small mint sprigs, to garnish

1 Melt the butter in a skillet. Add the onion, and fry gently 5 minutes, until soft and lightly colored.

2 Pour in the broth and bring to a boil, then add the peas, reserved pods, beans, mint sprig and salt and pepper to taste. Lower the heat, cover and simmer 20 minutes.

3 Remove the pods and mint sprig, leave the soup to cool slightly, then work in a blender or food processor until smooth. Or work through the medium blade of a vegetable mill. Leave until completely cold.

4 Mix the yogurt in a bowl with the curry paste and garlic, if using, then beat in about 6 tablespoons of the soup until smooth. Stir the

yogurt mixture into the soup, making sure that it is well mixed in. Refrigerate for at least 30 minutes.

5 To serve: Pour the soup into 4 chilled individual soup bowls and float a mint sprig on top of each.

Cook's Notes

TIME
Preparation and cooking take 70 minutes, but allow extra time for cooling and chilling.

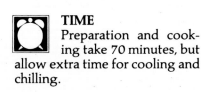

VARIATIONS
Frozen peas and beans may be used. In this case, you will need ¾ lb of peas and ½ lb of beans. Do not thaw them before cooking.

To serve the soup hot, make up to the end of stage 3, but do not cool. Pour into a saucepan, heat gently without boiling, then stir in the yogurt mixture. Garnish with chopped mint.

FREEZING
Pour the cooled soup in to a rigid container, seal, label and freeze for 6-8 weeks. To serve: thaw for 6-8 hours in the refrigerator,

stirring occasionally. If too thick, stir in a little cold milk.

COOK'S TIP
Pea pods have a deliciously strong pea taste. They are too fibrous and stringy to be included in a soup, but if added during the first part of cooking and them removed, they will add extra flavor.

● 150 calories per portion

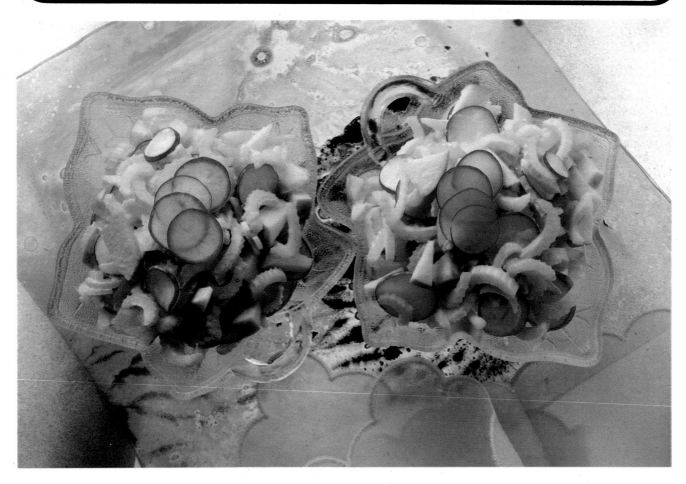

Celery and radish salad

SERVES 4

1 crisp dessert apple
1 small head celery, finely chopped
½ lb radishes, thinly sliced (see Buying guide)
salt and freshly ground black pepper

DRESSING

¼ cup ricotta cheese
4 tablespoons dairy sour cream
2 tablespoons cider vinegar
1 teaspoon firmly packed light brown sugar
1 clove garlic, crushed (optional)

1 Make the dressing: Put the cheese into a large bowl and beat until softened. Gradually beat in the sour cream and vinegar, then the sugar and garlic, if using.

2 Core and finely chop (but do not pare) the apple. Add to the dressing with the celery and half the radishes. Mix well, and season.

3 Transfer the salad to a serving bowl and arrange the remaining radishes on top in an attractive pattern. Serve as soon as possible, at room temperature.

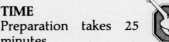

Cook's Notes

TIME
Preparation takes 25 minutes.

VARIATIONS
Cream cheese may be used instead of the ricotta and plain yogurt instead of dairy sour cream.

BUYING GUIDE
The average bunch of radishes available from vegetable stores weighs about ¼ lb so you will need 2 bunches for this recipe.

SERVING IDEAS
This salad goes perfectly with a quiche for lunch, or with cold chicken or turkey. It also makes an attractive appetizer salad as shown in the photograph, served with Melba toast and butter.

DID YOU KNOW
Celery is rich in mineral salts, vitamins and iron, and is one of the best vegetables for slimmers.

● 70 calories per portion

Cauliflower salad with sultanas

SERVES 6

1 cauliflower, broken into flowerets
1 lb baby white onions (see Preparation)
salt
1 cup white wine
½ cup water
5 tablespoons olive oil
2 tablespoons wine vinegar
3 tomatoes, peeled, seeded and chopped
3 tablespoons golden raisins
1 teaspoon firmly packed light brown sugar
½ teaspoon dried thyme
½ teaspoon ground coriander
freshly ground black pepper

1 Bring 2 pans of salted water to the boil and blanch the cauliflower and the onion separately 5 minutes. Drain both together in a strainer, then rinse under cold running water to refresh. Drain the vegetables again.

2 Put the remaining ingredients in a large pan with salt to taste and a generous sprinkling of black pepper. Stir well to mix, bring to the boil and boil 5 minutes.

3 Lower the heat, add the cauliflower and onions and simmer a further 8 minutes. [!]

4 Using a slotted spoon, transfer the vegetables to a serving dish. Bring the sauce left in the pan to the boil and boil 5 minutes to reduce slightly. Pour the sauce over the vegetables and leave until cold. Serve at room temperature.

Cook's Notes

TIME
Preparation 10 minutes, cooking about 20 minutes, but allow time for cooling the salad before serving.

WATCHPOINT
Be careful not to overcook the cauliflower flowerets. Test with the point of a knife during cooking to check that they are still crisp.

PREPARATION
Cut off the ends of the onions and remove the skins: keep the onions whole.

SERVING IDEAS
This is an ideal dish for an appetizer as it can be prepared in advance. Serve with warm bread.

● 175 calories per portion

Crunchy mixed salad

SERVES 4

¼ large cucumber
10 oz beansprouts (see Buying guide)
6 oz green grapes
1 small onion, thinly sliced

DRESSING

2 oz mild Cheddar cheese
2 tablespoons vegetable oil
1 tablespoon white wine vinegar
½ teaspoon Dijon-style mustard
¼ teaspoon sugar
salt and freshly ground black pepper

1 Pare the cucumber, cut it in half lengthwise, then scoop out the pits (see Preparation and Cook's tip). Cut into matchstick strips about 2-inches long and pat dry on paper towels.

2 Wash the beansprouts well under cold running water and drain well on paper towels.

3 Cut the grapes in half, or quarter them if large, and remove the pits with the point of a sharp knife.

4 Make the dressing: Crumble the cheese finely into a large bowl. Beat in the oil, vinegar, mustard, sugar and salt and pepper to taste.

5 Add the cucumber, beansprouts, onions and grapes to the dressing and toss well to combine. Cover and leave to stand 10 minutes to allow the flavors to blend.

6 Just before serving, toss the salad to gather up the juices.

Cook's Notes

TIME
Preparation takes about 40 minutes including standing time.

PREPARATION
To remove the pits from the cucumber:

Scoop out the pits from each half with a teaspoon.

SERVING IDEAS
The salad goes well with canned fish such as tuna or mackerel.

BUYING GUIDE
Beansprouts are often sold in supermarkets in 10 oz packages. Eat beansprouts within 2 days of buying to ensure freshness.

COOK'S TIP
Removing the cucumber pits helps to reduce the moisture which can dilute salad dressing.

● 155 calories per portion

Waldorf salad

SERVES 4

1 lb crisp dessert apples
(see Buying guide)
2 tablespoons lemon juice
1 teaspoon sugar
⅔ cup thick mayonnaise
½ head of celery,
chopped
½ cup shelled walnuts, chopped
(see Economy)
1 Bibb lettuce, leaves separated
(optional)

1 Quarter and core the apples but do not pare them, cut into neat dice and put into a bowl. Add the lemon juice and toss well to prevent coloration.

2 Stir in the sugar and 1 tablespoon of the mayonnaise. Mix until the apple is well coated, then leave in a cool place until ready to serve.

3 Just before serving, add the remaining mayonnaise, celery and walnuts and toss well together.

4 Place the prepared apple mixture in a bowl lined, if liked, with lettuce leaves. Serve at once.

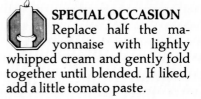

Cook's Notes

TIME
15 minutes advance preparation, then 5 minutes preparation before serving.

BUYING GUIDE
To add color to the salad, select red-skinned apples or buy half red and half green.

SERVING IDEAS
Serve as an accompaniment to cold meats or as part of a buffet selection. For a more decorative finish, add a border of thinly-sliced apples sprinkled with lemon juice, and garnish with a few whole walnuts.

DID YOU KNOW
This salad is so-called because it was first created by the chef of the Waldorf-Astoria Hotel in New York City.

ECONOMY
Buy packages of broken walnuts or walnut pieces; they are always less expensive than whole nuts.

SPECIAL OCCASION
Replace half the mayonnaise with lightly whipped cream and gently fold together until blended. If liked, add a little tomato paste.

● 355 calories per portion

31

Piquant zucchini salad

SERVES 4

4 large zucchini, trimmed
1 small red pepper, seeded and finely chopped
1-2 tablespoons drained capers
1 tablespoon finely chopped fresh parsley
1 lettuce, leaves separated, to serve

DRESSING
2 tablespoons vegetable oil
1 tablespoon lemon juice
pinch of superfine sugar
pinch of dry mustard
salt and freshly ground black pepper

1 Quarter the zucchini lengthwise, then cut them into ½-inch slices. Put them in a bowl with the red pepper, capers and parsley and mix together with a metal spoon (see Cook's tips).
2 Put the dressing ingredients in a small bowl with salt and pepper to taste, and beat together with a fork. Pour the dressing over the zucchini mixture and stir with a metal spoon until evenly coated.
3 To serve: Line 4 individual salad bowls with the lettuce leaves, then pile the zucchini mixture in the center of each lettuce-lined bowl just before the salads are to be served (see Cook's tips).

Cook's Notes

TIME
Preparation of this simple salad takes 15-20 minutes.

COOK'S TIPS
Use a metal rather than a wooden spoon to help prevent the zucchini slices from breaking up.
The zucchini mixture and dressing can be stirred together as much as 1 hour before serving. Stir the mixture again and spoon it into the lettuce-lined bowls at the last minute.

SERVING IDEAS
Serve as a light appetizer, or as an accompaniment to plainly cooked hot meat or fish dishes.

● 90 calories per portion

Tomato and mozzarella salad

SERVES 6

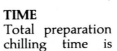

1 lb firm ripe tomatoes, cut into
¼-inch slices
2 tablespoons chopped fresh
parsley
2 tablespoons chopped fresh basil
or ½ teaspoon dried basil
pinch of sugar
salt and freshly ground black pepper
6 oz mozzarella cheese, cut into
¼-inch slices (see
Did you know)
3 tablespoons black olives
4 tablespoons olive oil

1 Arrange the tomato slices in an overlapping circular pattern around a flat serving dish. Sprinkle over the herbs and sugar and season with salt and pepper to taste. Cover the dish loosely with foil and chill in the refrigerator 30 minutes.
2 Remove the foil and arrange the cheese slices in the center of the tomatoes. scatter the olives over.
3 Just before serving, pour over the olive oil and, using a fork, gently lift up the tomato slices so that the oil drains through to them. Serve at once.

Cook's Notes

TIME
Total preparation and chilling time is 45 minutes.

DID YOU KNOW
Mozzarella cheese comes from southern Italy. Originally made from buffalo milk, but nowadays usually made with cow's milk, it is mild and moist, with a very definite flavor. It is available from specialty food stores.

SERVING IDEAS
This classic Italian tomato salad, which is dressed with oil alone, and not the more usual oil and vinegar dressing, makes a good accompaniment to roast and broiled meats. Serve it with pork chops or steak or, for a change, with roast or broiled chicken. Well chilled, it also makes a refreshing, easy-to-prepare first course.

● 205 calories per portion

Chinese beansprout salad

SERVES 4

½ large cucumber, pared
½ lb beansprouts
2 oz turnip greens, stems removed and finely shredded
¼ cup roasted peanuts
salt and freshly ground black pepper

DRESSING
2 oz Danish Blue cheese
6 tablespoons vegetable oil
2 tablespoons wine vinegar
a little milk (optional)

1 Cut the cucumber into 1½-inch lengths, then cut these lengthwise into thin sticks. Place in a salad bowl with the beansprouts.
2 Add the turnip greens and mix all the vegetables together.
3 Make the dressing: Crumble the blue cheese into a bowl and mash with a fork. Add the oil a little at a time, mixing it into the cheese with the fork to form a paste. Mix in the vinegar and add a little milk if the mixture seems too thick for a dressing (see Cook's tips).
4 Just before serving, add the peanuts to the salad and pour over the dressing. ⚠ Toss until all the ingre-

dients are thoroughly coated in the dressing, then add salt and pepper to taste. Serve at once while the beansprouts and nuts are crunchy.

Cook's Notes

TIME
Preparation takes about 20 minutes.

VARIATIONS
Try using any one of the other blue cheeses available in supermarkets, such as Stilton.

SERVING IDEAS
Serve as a side dish with beef casseroles, hot roast lamb or broiled white fish.
Alternatively, serve as a first course in individual bowls, topped with garlic-flavored croutons (small cubes of bread fried in oil to which 2 crushed garlic cloves have been added).

COOK'S TIPS
If you have a blender or food processor, put all the ingredients in the machine

together and work until smooth.
You can prepare the salad ingredients and dressing separately, several hours in advance of serving. Store in covered plastic containers in the refrigerator and combine together with peanuts just before serving.

SPECIAL OCCASION
If you are feeling extravagant, for a dinner party or special occasion, use the French blue cheese, Roquefort, available from delicatessens and specialty food stores.

WATCHPOINT
Add the peanuts at the last minute, just before you dress the salad, so that they do not lose their crunchiness.

● 345 calories per portion

Crisp and crunchy salad

SERVES 4

6 oz white cabbage, coarsely shredded
6 oz red cabbage, finely shredded
1 large carrot, finely grated
2 celery stalks, chopped
1 small green pepper, seeded and finely chopped
4 oz fresh beansprouts (optional, see Buying guide)
½ cup salted peanuts

DRESSING

4 oz blue cheese
⅔ cup olive oil
3 tablespoons wine vinegar
½ teaspoon made English mustard
2 tablespoons chopped chives
salt and freshly ground black pepper

1 Put the cabbage in a large salad bowl (use a glass one, if possible) with the carrot, celery, green pepper and beansprouts, if using.

2 Make the dressing: Using a fork, mash the cheese in a small bowl. When it is smooth, add the olive oil a little at a time, and continue mixing until creamy.

3 Add the vinegar and mix in until combined, then stir in the mustard and chives, and salt and pepper to taste.

4 Just before serving, add the peanuts to the salad in the bowl, then pour over the dressing and stir well to mix. [!] Serve as soon as possible.

Cook's Notes

TIME
This salad takes 30 minutes to prepare.

COOK'S TIP
Try to shred the 2 cabbages to different thicknesses. The different textures add interest to the salad.

WATCHPOINT
Do not add the peanuts until just before you mix in the dressing otherwise they will become soft.

VARIATIONS
Add or subtract the ingredients according to what you have available. Keep a balance of colors and crisp ingredients. Use any of the cheeses such as Danish Blue or Stilton.

SERVING IDEAS
Serve as a main course for a healthy lunch — there is plenty of protein in the nuts and cheese to balance all the vegetables.

BUYING GUIDE
Buy fresh beansprouts, if they are available, and use the same day. Canned beansprouts are unsuitable as they are not crisp.

● 600 calories per portion

Pea and bean salad

SERVES 4

¾ lb peas (weighed in the pod), shelled, or ¾ cup frozen peas
⅓ cup dried red kidney beans, soaked overnight, or 1 can (about 8 oz) red kidney beans
1 lb lima beans (weighed in the pod), shelled, or ¼ lb frozen lima beans
salt
1 small red pepper, seeded and finely chopped
1 small green pepper, seeded and finely chopped
1 bunch scallions, finely chopped
2 tablespoons chopped parsley

FRENCH DRESSING

3 tablespoons olive oil
1 tablespoon lemon juice
1 tablespoon white wine or wine vinegar
1 teaspoon mild Dijon-style mustard
1 teaspoon superfine sugar
freshly ground black pepper

1 Drain the soaked kidney beans, cook in boiling water about 1 hour until tender (see Cook's tips), then drain and cool slightly. If using canned beans, drain off the liquid from the can, then rinse the beans thoroughly under cold running water.

2 Cook the fresh lima beans and peas in separate pans of boiling salted water until just tender (5-7 minutes). If using frozen beans and peas, cook according to package directions. Drain and cool slightly.

3 Mix together the beans, peas, red and green peppers, scallions and chopped parsley in a bowl.

4 To make the French dressing: Place all the ingredients in a screw-top jar with salt and pepper to taste. Replace the lid firmly and shake well to mix.

5 Pour the French dressing over the bean mixture and toss well until all the vegetables are thoroughly coated. Taste and adjust seasoning. Cover the bowl with plastic wrap, then refrigerate about 2 hours. Transfer to a salad bowl before serving.

Cook's Notes

TIME
Soak red kidney beans overnight then cook 1 hour. Preparation of the other vegetables 20-30 minutes, and cooking about 5-7 minutes. Chill salad for at least 2 hours.

COOK'S TIPS
The kidney beans *must* boil vigorously for a good 10 minutes, and then simmer for the rest of the cooking time. Do not add salt to the cooking water; it toughens the skins.

SERVING IDEAS
This makes a delicious snack lunch on its own with whole wheat rolls. It goes well with all cold meat, particularly beef, and makes a colorful addition to a buffet spread. Serve it, too, as part of a vegetarian meal.

PRESSURE COOKING
The kidney beans will cook in 20 minutes in a pressure cooker at high pressure.

● 195 calories per portion

Avocado and grapefruit salad

SERVES 4

2 small avocados
1 small grapefruit
2 dessert apples

1 small lettuce, separated into
  leaves

DRESSING
1 tablespoon clear honey
2 tablespoons cider vinegar
6 tablespoons olive oil
salt and freshly ground black pepper

1 To make the dressing: Mix together the honey, vinegar and olive oil in a bowl. Beat with a fork until the dressing is thick and all the ingredients are thoroughly combined. Season to taste.
2 Peel the grapefruit. Hold it over a bowl to catch the juice and, using a small, sharp knife, trim away any white pith. Divide the grapefruit into sections and remove the pips. Stir the sections into the dressing.
3 Halve the avocados lengthwise, remove the seeds and pare. Slice the flesh and add immediately to the dressing. [!] Toss thoroughly.
4 Quarter and core the apples. Slice them thinly and toss them in the dressing. Taste and adjust seasoning. Arrange the lettuce leaves in a salad bowl, pile the salad in the center and serve at once.

Cook's Notes

TIME
This salad takes 15 minutes to make.

WATCHPOINT
Always assemble this salad just before you wish to serve it, although you can make the dressing in advance and store in a covered container. The reason is that avocados tend to color slightly once they have been sliced even when incorporated in the dressing.
Also the dressing itself will make the lettuce limp if it is poured over too soon.

VARIATIONS
Use 2 large oranges in place of grapefruit. If you cannot buy cider vinegar, use white wine vinegar.

SERVING IDEAS
To make a light lunch or supper dish, serve this salad with cottage cheese or tuna fish.

● 450 calories per portion

Brussels sprouts and date salad

SERVES 6

1 lb Brussels sprouts
½ lb carrots, grated
⅔ cup chopped pitted dates

DRESSING

⅔ cup plain yogurt, chilled
2 tablespoons mayonnaise
2 tablespoons fresh orange juice
salt and freshly ground black pepper
2 tablespoons chopped chives

TO SERVE

2 heads Belgian endive or 1 lettuce heart, trimmed and separated into leaves
¼ cup walnut halves (optional)

1 Trim the sprouts, discarding any tough or colored outer leaves. Wash and drain them thoroughly, tossing them in a clean dish cloth or on paper towels.

2 Shred the sprouts with a sharp knife, then place in a large mixing bowl with the grated carrots and dates. Mix well to combine.

3 To make the dressing: Beat together the yogurt, mayonnaise and orange juice. Add salt and pepper to taste, then stir in the chives.

4 Pour the dressing over the vegetables and mix well. Taste and adjust seasoning. Cover and refrigerate about 1 hour, or longer.

5 To serve: Line a deep serving bowl with the endive or lettuce leaves, then spoon the chilled salad into the center, piling it up in a mound. Garnish with walnuts, if using.

Gazpacho salad

SERVES 4
¾ lb tomatoes, peeled and thinly
    sliced
½ large cucumber, pared and thinly
    sliced
1 medium onion, thinly sliced
1 medium red pepper, seeded and
    thinly sliced
1 medium green pepper, seeded and
    thinly sliced
salt, freshly ground black pepper
    and sugar
10 tablespoons white or brown
    bread crumbs
8 tablespoons French dressing (see
    Cook's tips)

TO SERVE
10 black olives
1 tablespoon chopped parsley

1 Prepare the tomatoes, cucumber,
onion and peppers as indicated
above. Plunge the peppers in boiling water for 30 seconds (to blanch),
and then immerse them immediately
in cold water (to refresh them).
2 In a glass bowl, put a layer of
cucumber, followed by a layer of
tomatoes and a sprinkling of sugar,
a layer of onion and a layer of mixed
red and green peppers. Season with
salt and pepper and sprinkle over 2
tablespoons bread crumbs and 2
tablespoons French dressing.
3 Continue these layers, finishing
with a layer of 4 tablespoons bread
crumbs. Cover these with French
dressing so that they are well
soaked, then cover the bowl with
plastic wrap and refrigerate for 2-3
hours before actually serving.

Cook's Notes

TIME
The preparation of the
salad should take no
longer than 20 minutes, but
remember you should allow 2-3
hours chilling time in the
refrigerator before the gazpacho salad is ready to serve.

COOK'S TIPS
This is a salad version
of the better known
gazpacho soup. A French dressing well-flavored with garlic is
really essential. Mix together 6
tablespoons olive oil and 2
tablespoons wine vinegar (or
lemon juice) and season with
freshly ground black pepper.
Crush a garlic clove with salt
using the blade of a small knife,
and blend it into the dressing.
(Use only half a clove if your
family prefers a mild garlic
flavor). Vegetables are blanched
for a variety of reasons — to
soften them before further
cooking, to retain color, to get
rid of a bitter flavor. Refreshing
immediately in cold water stops
any further cooking.

SERVING IDEAS
The salad goes particu-
larly well with plain
broiled or barbecued meat. It is
also a good accompaniment to
simple, fried hamburgers.

● 185 calories per portion

Leek and potato pie

SERVES 4

1 lb leeks
salt
1½ lb potatoes
3 tablespoons butter or margarine
2 tablespoons all-purpose flour
1¼ cups warm milk
pinch of freshly grated nutmeg
freshly ground black pepper
½ cup grated Cheddar cheese
butter, for greasing

1 Trim the leeks, discarding most of the dark green part (see Economy). Slice thickly and wash under cold running water until completely clean. Cook in boiling salted water 8-10 minutes or until almost tender. Drain thoroughly, reserving the broth.

2 At the same time, cook the potatoes in boiling salted water about 20-25 minutes or until tender. Drain.

3 While the vegetables are cooking, make sauce: Melt 2 tablespoons of butter gently in a small saucepan, sprinkle in the flour and stir over a low heat 2 minutes until straw-colored. Remove from the heat and gradually stir in all but 2 tablespoons of the milk, then return to the heat and simmer, stirring, until thick and smooth. Measure out about ⅔ cup of the leek broth (see Economy); stir gradually into white sauce. Bring back to a boil, stirring constantly, then add the nutmeg and salt and pepper to taste. Remove the pan from the heat.

4 Preheat the oven to 375°.

5 Slice one-third of the potatoes, stir them gently into the leeks and turn into the base of a greased 5 cup ovenproof dish. Pour on the sauce; carefully turn vegetables with a fork, to coat thoroughly.

6 Add remaining butter and milk to the rest of the potatoes, season with pepper, then mash them until smooth. Beat in half the

cheese with a wooden spoon. Taste and adjust seasoning.

7 Spread the mashed potato over the vegetables, then sprinkle on the

rest of the cheese. Stand the dish on a cookie sheet and bake in the oven 20-25 minutes, or until the topping is golden brown. Serve hot.

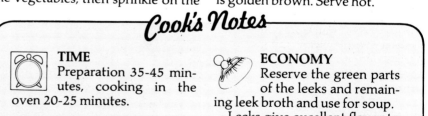

Cook's Notes

TIME
Preparation 35-45 minutes, cooking in the oven 20-25 minutes.

SERVING IDEAS
Serve with fried or boiled bacon or any cold cooked meat.

ECONOMY
Reserve the green parts of the leeks and remaining leek broth and use for soup.
Leeks give excellent flavor to a vegetable soup. Remember to wash trimmings thoroughly.

● 390 calories per portion

Vegetable pie

SERVES 4-6

1 cup all-purpose flour
salt
¼ cup butter or margarine, diced
½ cup grated Cheddar cheese
about 4 teaspoons chilled water
beaten egg or milk, for glazing

FILLING

1 lb potatoes, diced
3 carrots, sliced
3 leeks, cut into ½-inch slices
1 tablespoon chopped fresh parsley
freshly ground black pepper
2 tablespoons butter or margarine
2 tablespoons all-purpose flour
1¼ cups vegetable or chicken broth

1 Make the pastry: Sift the flour and a pinch of salt into a bowl. Add the butter and cut it into the flour until all the mixture resembles fine crumbs.

2 Mix in the grated cheese and just enough cold water to draw the mixture together to a firm dough. Wrap in plastic wrap and refrigerate 30 minutes.

3 Preheat the oven to 350°. Meanwhile, make the filling: Cook the potatoes and carrots in boiling salted water 10 minutes. Drain thoroughly, then place vegetables in 3¾ cup pie dish with leeks, mixing them well together. Sprinkle with the pastry and salt and pepper to taste. Set aside.

4 Melt the butter in a clean saucepan, sprinkle in the flour and stir over a low heat 1-2 minutes until straw-colored. Gradually stir in the broth, then bring to a boil and simmer, stirring, until thick and smooth. Pour over the vegetables.

5 Roll out the pastry on a floured surface to a shape slightly larger than the top of the pie dish. Cut off a long strip of pastry all around the edge. Reserve this and other trimmings. Brush the rim of the pie dish with water, then press the narrow strip of pastry all around the rim. Brush the strip with a little more water, then place the large piece of pastry on top. Press to seal, then trim, knock up and crimp the edge of the pie.

6 Make decorations from the trimmings, brush the undersides with water and place on top of the pie. Brush the pastry lid with a little beaten egg, and make a hole in the center. Bake in the oven 40-45 minutes until the pastry is golden brown and the vegetables are tender. Serve at once.

Cook's Notes

TIME
1½ hours preparation and cooking time, including chilling the cheese shortcrust pastry.

VARIATIONS
The vegetables may be replaced by whatever is in season.

Instead of the cheese pastry crust, use 1 sheet (½ of 17 oz package) frozen puff pastry.

● 425 calories per portion

Zucchini bake

SERVES 4-6

1 lb small zucchini, cut into
   1-inch lengths (see
   Buying guide)
2 tablespoons butter or margarine
1 onion, chopped
salt
3 eggs, beaten
¾ cup grated Cheddar cheese
⅔ cup milk
2 tablespoons chopped fresh
   parsley
good pinch of freshly grated
   nutmeg
freshly ground black pepper
butter, for greasing

1 Preheat the oven to 350° and grease an 8½-inch flan dish, about 1½-inches deep, with the butter.

2 Melt the butter in a skillet, add the onion and cook gently 10 minutes until browned. Remove the pan from the heat and cool.

3 meanwhile, bring a saucepan of lightly salted water to a boil. Add the zucchini and simmer for 5 minutes. Drain thoroughly and then set aside.

4 Mix the eggs, cheese, milk, parsley and nutmeg together in a bowl. Season to taste with salt and pepper then stir in the onion.

5 Stand the pieces of zucchini upright in the flan dish, then carefully spoon in the egg mixture, making sure it is evenly distributed.

6 Bake the custard in the oven about 40 minutes until it is set and the top is golden brown. Leave to stand for about 10 minutes before serving, cut into wedges.

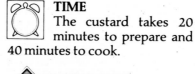

Cook's Notes

TIME
The custard takes 20 minutes to prepare and 40 minutes to cook.

VARIATION
Chervil may be used instead of parsley.

SERVING IDEAS
This custard makes an unusual vegetable accompaniment to plainly broiled meat. You may find that because of the large amount of zucchini used you will not need an additional vegetable.

BUYING GUIDE
Buy the smallest zucchini you can find — there should be 6-9 to 1 lb.

● 230 calories per portion

Vegetable crumble

SERVES 4

2 leeks, cut into ½-inch slices (see Preparation)
2 tablespoons olive oil or sunflower oil
2 large carrots, thickly sliced
1 small red pepper, seeded and diced
1 lb zucchini, cut into ½-inch slices
1 can (about 14 oz) tomatoes
½ teaspoon dried basil
salt and freshly ground black pepper
about ½ cup pine nuts (see Buying guide)
2 teaspoons wine vinegar

CRUMBLE TOPPING

1 cup all-purpose or whole wheat flour
¼ teaspoon salt
3 tablespoons butter, diced
½ cup grated fresh Parmesan cheese, (see Buying guide)

1 Heat the oil in a large saucepan, add the leeks and carrots and cook over moderate heat 5 minutes. stirring. Add the red pepper and cook 5 minutes, then add the zucchini and cook a further 5 minutes, stirring constantly.

2 Add the tomatoes and their juices to the pan with the basil and salt and pepper to taste. Bring to a boil, then lower the heat, cover and simmer 10 minutes.

3 Meanwhile, preheat the oven to 400° and then make the crumble: Sift the flour and salt into a bowl. Add the butter and cut slowly into the flour until all the mixture resembles fine bread crumbs. Stir in most of the Parmesan, and then add pepper to taste.

4 Add the pine nuts and vinegar to vegetables, then transfer to a 1½ quart casserole. Sprinkle the crumble evenly over vegetables, then top with remaining Parmesan.

5 Bake in the oven about 40 minutes, until golden.

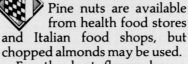

TIME
Preparation time 30-40 minutes, then about 40 minutes baking.

PREPARATION
Wash the leeks, then slice them and put into a strainer. Rinse again under cold running water, to remove any remaining grit and dirt.

BUYING GUIDE
Pine nuts are available from health food stores and Italian food shops, but chopped almonds may be used.

For the best flavor, buy a whole piece of Parmesan and grate it yourself at home when needed. Tightly wrapped in plastic wrap it will keep its flavor for several weeks in the refrigerator. Special graters for this hard cheese can be bought from some kitchen and hardware shops.

If you do not want to go to the trouble of grating the cheese yourself, buy freshly grated Parmesan from an Italian delicatessen; do not buy packages or tubs of grated Parmesan from a supermarket for this dish.

●390 calories per portion

Vegetable fried rice

SERVES 4

1⅓ cups long-grain rice
salt
½ lb carrots, diced
1 parsnip, diced
1 small turnip, diced
2 tablespoons vegetable oil
1 large onion, chopped
1 clove garlic, crushed (optional)
½ cup sliced mushrooms
2 large tomatoes, peeled and sliced
⅓ cup frozen peas, thawed
freshly ground black pepper
2 eggs, lightly beaten
1 tablespoon chopped fresh parsley
grated Parmesan cheese, to serve

1 Bring a large saucepan of salted water to a boil, add the rice and cover. Lower the heat and simmer 10 minutes, or until the rice is just tender.
2 Meanwhile, bring another pan of salted water to the boil. Add the carrots, parsnip and turnip and cover. Lower the heat and cook about 8-10 minutes, or until all the vegetables are barely tender.
3 Drain the cooked root vegetables and reserve. Drain the rice in a strainer and rinse well under hot running water to separate the grains. Drain again.
4 Heat the oil in a large non-stick saucepan, add the onion and garlic, if using, and cook gently 5 minutes, or until the onion is soft and lightly colored.
5 Add the drained root vegetables to the pan, together with the mushrooms, tomatoes, peas and rice. Stir well and season to taste with salt and plenty of pepper. Cover the pan and cook over very low heat 10 minutes. ✳
6 Stir in the eggs and gently turn the mixture so that the egg cooks. Remove from the heat and turn into a warmed serving dish. Garnish with the parsley and serve at once with the Parmesan cheese.

Cook's Notes

TIME
This dish will take about 35 minutes to make.

 VARIATIONS
Small, partly-cooked cauliflower flowerets or broccoli make tasty alternatives to the root vegetables used here — and their shape adds a pleasant variation, too.
Make the dish even more substantial by adding about ½ cup chopped, cooked ham or cooked chicken at the beginning of stage 5.

FREEZING
Cool completely and pack into a rigid container. Seal, label and freeze for up to 2 months. To serve: Allow to thaw overnight in the refrigerator. Reheat very gently and stir in the eggs just before serving.

 SERVING IDEAS
This dish makes an excellent accompaniment to meat dishes. Or serve with tomato sauce on its own.

● 410 calories per portion

Potato pizza

SERVES 4

1 cup self-rising flour
salt
¼ cup butter or margarine
1 cup cold mashed potatoes
vegetable oil, for greasing

TOPPING

1 tablespoon vegetable oil
1 large onion, sliced
1 red pepper, seeded and sliced
1 clove garlic (optional)
    (optional
1 cup sliced small mushrooms
pinch of oregano
2 teaspoons vinegar
freshly ground black pepper
1 tablespoon tomato paste
6 oz Cheddar cheese, sliced

1 Preheat the oven to 450°. Oil a large cookie sheet.

2 Make the base: Sift the flour and salt into a large bowl. Add the butter and cut it in until all the mixture resembles bread crumbs, then add the mashed potatoes and knead the mixture lightly until smooth.

3 Press the dough into a 10-inch round and refrigerate.

4 Meanwhile, make the topping: Heat the oil in a skillet, add the onion, red pepper and garlic, if using, and cook gently 5 minutes or until the onion is soft and lightly colored. Remove the pan from the heat and stir in the mushrooms, oregano, vinegar and salt and pepper to taste.

5 Place the potato base on the cookie sheet and spread the tomato paste over it, then top with the onion mixture. Arrange the cheese slices over the top.

6 Bake in the oven 25-30 minutes or until the base is firm and the cheese is golden brown.

Cook's Notes

TIME
Preparation takes about 40 minutes, including preparing the potatoes; allow time for chilling. Cooking takes 25-30 minutes.

SERVING IDEAS
This delicious pizza makes an excellent supper dish served with a green salad and French bread.

VARIATIONS
For a more Italian flavor, top the cheese with anchovy fillets, slices of salami and black olives, then drizzle with a little olive oil to prevent drying out. Mozzarella cheese can be used instead of Cheddar.

● 500 calories per portion

Red summer flan

 SERVES 4-6

½ lb red peppers, seeded and cut
    into thin slices
¾ lb tomatoes, thinly sliced
2 tablespoons vegetable oil
4 cloves garlic, crushed
½ cup fresh white bread crumbs
½ teaspoon dried basil
salt and freshly ground black pepper
1 teaspoon sugar

PASTRY
1½ cups all-purpose flour
pinch of salt
¼ cup butter, diced
2 tablespoons shortening, diced
½ cup finely grated Cheddar cheese
½ teaspoon dried mixed herbs
2 tablespoons cold water
lightly beaten egg white, to seal

1 Preheat the oven to 400°.
2 Make the pastry: Sift the flour and salt into a bowl. Add the butter and fat and cut in until the mixture resembles fine bread crumbs. Stir in the grated cheese and herbs, then add the cold water and mix to a fairly firm dough.
3 Turn the dough out onto a lightly floured surface and roll out thinly. Use to line a 8-9 inch flan ring, set on a cookie sheet, prick the base with a fork. Place a large circle of waxed paper or foil in the pie shell and weight it down with baking beans. Bake 10 minutes.
4 Remove the paper or foil lining and beans, brush the inside of the pie shell with beaten egg white, then return the pastry to the oven a further 5 minutes. Remove from the oven and set aside.
5 Make the filling: Heat the oil in a skillet, add the peppers and cook gently 5 minutes until beginning to soften. Add the garlic and continue to cook until soft and lightly colored. Set aside.
6 Put the bread crumbs in a bowl with the basil and salt and pepper to taste. Mix well.
7 Spread the peppers over the base of the pie shell, then cover with the tomto slices. Sprinkle with sugar, then finish with a layer of the bread crumb mixture.
8 Bake in the oven 30-35 minutes until the tomatoes are tender and the pastry is golden.
9 Serve the flan hot or cold.

Cook's Notes

TIME
35 minutes to prepare and bake the pie shell; about 50 minutes to finish.

SERVING IDEAS
This colorful flan makes a satisfying lunch or supper dish. Serve hot with a fresh green vegetable and new potatoes, or serve cold with a mixed green salad.

VARIATION
To cut down on preparation time, use about ½ lb of pie crust sticks.

Canned peppers may be used instead of fresh peppers—there is no need to cook them, simply drain, slice and stir into the cooked garlic.

● 395 calories per slice

Spinach fried with mushrooms

SERVES 4

¼ cup butter
1 lb spinach, stems and large midribs removed, shredded (see Watchpoint)
2 cups sliced mushrooms
½ teaspoon freshly grated nutmeg
salt and freshly ground black pepper
4 tablespoons dairy sour cream

1 Melt the butter in a heavy saucepan or flameproof casserole. Add the spinach, sliced mushrooms and nutmeg and season to taste with salt and pepper. Cover the pan and cook over a very low heat 8-10 minutes until the vegetables are just cooked. Stir frequently during this time to ensure even cooking.

2 Transfer the vegetables to a warmed serving dish and drizzle dairy sour cream over top in an attractive pattern. Serve at once while still hot.

Cook's Notes

TIME
Preparation and cooking take 20-25 minutes.

VARIATIONS
Light cream may be used as a substitute for dairy sour cream. Alternatively, to make the dish less expensive, omit the cream altogether and sprinkle with lemon juice before serving.

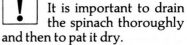**SERVING IDEAS**
Serve this quickly made dish as a vegetable accompaniment for 4, or as a light lunch dish for 2-3 people.

WATCHPOINT
It is important to drain the spinach thoroughly and then to pat it dry.

● 145 calories per portion

Leek and tomato casserole

SERVES 4-6

2 large leeks, trimmed, washed and
cut into 1 inch pieces (see
Preparation)
2 large onions, cut into eighths
1 can (about 14 oz) tomatoes
1 tablespoon chopped parsley
1 bay leaf
2 cloves garlic, crushed
(optional)
1 teaspoon salt
freshly ground black pepper
⅔ cup chicken or vegetable broth
4 tablespoons vegetable oil
1 tablespoon lemon juice
pinch of dried thyme

1 Preheat the oven to 350°.
2 Put all the ingredients into a large
bowl and mix well. Turn into a large
ovenproof dish or casserole, cover
and cook in the oven 1½-2 hours,
until tender. Serve hot.

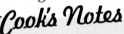

Cook's Notes

TIME
Preparation of vege-
tables 15 minutes, cook-
ing time in the oven 1½-2
hours.

ECONOMY
Save fuel by cooking
this dish with some-
thing else on the shelf below.

SERVING IDEAS
Serve this easy-to-make
vegetable dish on its
own or with roast beef or pork.

VARIATION
When tomatoes are
cheap and plentiful, use
fresh instead of canned, in
which case you may need a little
extra broth. Peel them before
mixing with other ingredients.

PREPARATION
Top and tails leeks; slit
them down almost to
base. Fan out under cold running water to rinse off all dirt.

● 175 calories per portion

Soy burgers

SERVES 4

¾ cup soybeans
2 tablespoons vegetable oil
1 onion, finely chopped
1 small carrot, grated
1 small green pepper, seeded and
    chopped
1 tablespoon tomato paste
1 teaspoon dried mixed herbs
salt
freshly ground black pepper
1 egg, beaten
1 tablespoon water
dried bread crumbs, for coating
vegetable oil, for frying

1 Put the beans into a bowl, cover with plenty of cold water and leave to soak overnight. Drain the soaked beans and put them into a saucepan; cover with cold water.
2 Bring the beans to a boil, then lower the heat and simmer over very gentle heat 3 hours until tender, topping up with more water if necessary. Transfer to a strainer and drain thoroughly.
3 Heat the oil in a skillet and gently cook the onion and carrot 5 minutes, until the onion is soft and lightly colored. Add the green pepper and cook a further 5 minutes, or until the vegetables are just tender.
4 Add the beans, tomato paste and herbs to the pan, mashing the beans with a spoon to make the mixture hold together. Season with salt and pepper to taste.
5 Divide the mixture into 8 and shape each piece into a neat, flat circle. Beat egg and water together in a shallow bowl and spread the bread crumbs out on a plate. Dip the burgers first into the beaten egg mixture, then into the dried bread crumbs, making sure they are well coated.
6 Heat the vegetable oil in a large skillet, add 4 burgers and cook over moderately high heat 3 minutes on each side until crisp and browned. Remove with a slotted spoon, place on a serving platter, and keep warm. Cook the remaining burgers in the same way and serve at once.

Cook's Notes

TIME
Allow for the overnight soaking of the beans, followed by 3 hours cooking. Preparation and cooking then take about 30 minutes.

PRESSURE COOKING
Soybeans can be cooked in a pressure-cooker. Soak and rinse as in the recipe, then cook at high (H) pressure for 1 hour.

FREEZING
Drained, cooked soy-beans can be frozen in plastic bags for use. Soy bean burgers can be frozen before cooking: open-freeze until solid, then pack in a rigid container, separating the layers with foil. Seal, label and return to the freezer for up to 2 months. To serve: Cook from frozen.

SERVING IDEAS
Serve the burgers with mashed potatoes or French fries and parsley sauce; or with chutney and soft rolls.

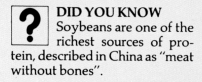

DID YOU KNOW
Soybeans are one of the richest sources of protein, described in China as "meat without bones".

● 360 calories per portion

Creamy spring vegetables

SERVES 4

1 small onion, sliced
2 large scallions cut into ½-inch
    slices
2 carrots, cut into ½-inch slices
¼ cup butter
1¼ cups hot chicken broth
pinch of superfine sugar
salt and freshly ground black
    pepper
½ lb lima beans
    (shelled weight)
1½ cups shelled peas
1 teaspoon cornstarch
6 tablespoons heavy cream
1 tablespoon chopped fresh parsley,
    to garnish (optional)

1 Melt the butter in a saucepan, add the sliced onion and scallions and cook over moderate heat 2 minutes. Add the sliced carrots and cook a further 2 minutes, stirring to coat thoroughly.

2 Pour the hot broth into the pan, add the sugar and salt and pepper to taste, then bring to a boil. Lower the heat, cover and simmer gently 10 minutes. Add the lima beans and simmer a further 5 minutes. Add the peas and continue simmering another 10 minutes, until all the vegetables are tender.

3 Put the cornstarch into a small bowl and stir in 1 tablespoon of the

hot vegetable broth from the pan. Stir to make a smooth paste, then pour back into the pan. Stir the contents of the pan over a low heat about 4-5 minutes, until the sauce thickens and clears. Stir in the cream and allow just to heat through.

4 Turn the vegetables with the sauce into a warmed serving dish. Sprinkle with parsley, if liked, and serve at once.

Cheesy cabbage pan-flan

SERVES 4

2 lb potatoes, quartered
salt
1 lb green cabbage, cored and shredded
1½ cups grated sharp Cheddar cheese (see Buying guide)
1 large egg, beaten
freshly ground black pepper
6–8 scallions, chopped
2 tablespoons shortening

1 Cook the potatoes in boiling salted water about 20 minutes or until tender.

2 Meanwhile, cook the cabbage in boiling salted water 5 minutes. Drain thoroughly.

3 Drain the potatoes well, then return them to the saucepan. Dry out over gentle heat, then mash with 1 cup of cheese, the beaten egg and plenty of salt and pepper. Stir in the cabbage and scallions.

4 Melt shortening in a large skillet over high heat and swirl it around to cover the base and sides. Add the potato and cabbage mixture and spread it out evenly. Cook 3 minutes or until underside is golden (see Cook's tip).

5 Sprinkle with the remaining cheese, then put under a moderate broiler about 5 minutes, until the top is golden brown. Serve at once straight from pan cut in wedges.

Cook's Notes

TIME
Total preparation and cooking time is about 30 minutes.

COOK'S TIP
To see if the underside of the dish is golden brown, gently lift up the edge with a spatula. The center will become brown before the outside, so take care not to let the center become burnt.

VARIATIONS
Traditionally this dish is made with left-over mashed potato and cooked Brussels sprouts. If you prefer the stronger flavor of sprouts, then use these instead of the cabbage. A dash of Worcestershire sauce is a good complement to the cheese. Add it when mashing the potatoes and, if liked, mix a few drops in with the grated cheese for the topping.

SERVING IDEAS
Serve as a vegetable with sausages, bacon, chops, etc., or add chopped left-over cooked meat such as ham or bacon to the cheesy cabbage pan-flan to make a more substantial dish.

BUYING GUIDE
Canadian Cheddar cheese has just the right amount of flavor to give a "kick" to the potatoes and cabbage.

● 510 calories per portion

Potato and radish crunch

SERVES 4

 1 lb new potatoes (see
    Buying guide)
 salt
¼ cup butter
3 thick slices white bread,
    crusts removed and cut
    into ½-inch dice
2-inch piece of cucumber, diced
6 radishes, thinly sliced
1 tablespoon dry roasted
    peanuts
1 teaspoon chopped chives
freshly ground black pepper
4 tablespoons dairy sour cream

1 Boil a saucepan of salted water
and cook the potatoes 15-20
minutes until just tender. ⚠ Drain
well and, when cool enough to
handle, cut into ½-inch dice. Leave
to cool completely.

2 To make the croutons: Melt the
butter in a skillet. When it is sizzling,
add the diced bread and cook
gently, turning as necessary, until
golden. Drain well on paper towels.
Leave to cool completely.

3 Place the diced potato, fried
croutons, cucumber, radishes, peanuts and chives into a bowl. Season
to taste with salt and pepper. Add
dairy sour cream and mix gently. ⚠
Serve at once.

Cook's Notes

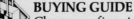

TIME
Preparation, including
cooking the potatoes
and frying the croutons, takes
about 30 minutes. Allow 30
minutes for cooling. Preparing
the salad takes 5 minutes.

BUYING GUIDE
Choose a firm type of
potato such as the red
or white new potatoes which
will not break up during
cooking.

WATCHPOINT
Watch the potatoes
carefully: they should
be cooked through but still firm.
If overcooked, they will break
up instead of cutting into neat
dice.

Mix gently so that the ingredients are thoroughly coated in
dairy sour cream but remain
separate.

VARIATIONS
Add a small chopped
green pepper instead of
cucumber.
Omit the peanuts and
sprinkle the top of the salad
with toasted, slivered almonds.

● 310 calories per portion

Potato 'n' tomato gratin

SERVES 4
1½ lb firm potatoes, sliced
salt
1¼ cups milk
1 cup grated Cheddar cheese

TOMATO SAUCE
3 tablespoons butter or margarine
1 medium onion, sliced
1 tablespoon all-purpose flour
1 can (about 14 oz) tomatoes
½ teaspoon sugar
1 teaspoon dried oregano
salt and freshly ground black pepper

1 Make sauce: Melt 2 tablespoons butter in a small saucepan, add the onion and cook gently 3 minutes, stirring occasionally. Do not allow the onion to brown. Sprinkle in the flour and cook 2 minutes, stirring constantly.

2 Add the tomatoes with their juice to the pan, stir in the sugar and oregano and season with salt and pepper to taste. Simmer 20 minutes until the tomato sauce has thickened, stirring occasionally.

3 Meanwhile, put the potatoes in a saucepan with the milk and ½ teaspoon salt. Bring slowly to a boil, then lower the heat and simmer uncovered 10-12 minutes. The potatoes should be tender when pierced with a fine skewer, but not beginning to break up. [!] Drain thoroughly.

4 Grease the inside of a shallow 3¾-4 cup flameproof dish with remaining butter, then arrange the potatoes in overlapping circles over the base.

5 Heat broiler to moderate. Taste and adjust seasoning of the tomato sauce. Pour over the potatoes ❋ and sprinkle the cheese over the top. Place the dish under broiler until the cheese topping is golden brown and bubbling. ❋ Serve the gratin very hot, straight from the dish.

Cook's Notes

⏰ TIME
Preparation 10 minutes. Boiling the potatoes, preparing sauce and browning takes 25 minutes.

❋ FREEZING
You can freeze the dish completely assembled, or without the cheese topping. Thaw at room temperature before broiling. Alternatively, cook it in the oven straight from the freezer: heat the oven to 375° and cook the dish 35-40 minutes or until the topping is golden brown.

[!] WATCHPOINT
Make sure that you cut the potatoes into even, thick slices and be careful not to overcook them as well. The dish would be very unattractive if made with squashy, moist potatoes. They must be in whole slices and still slightly firm.

VARIATION
Leeks, cooked till just tender and thoroughly drained, could be successfully used instead of the potatoes.

● 400 calories per portion

Bulgur wheat casserole

SERVES 4

8 oz bulgur wheat (see Did you know)
¼ cup butter or margarine
1 tablespoon vegetable oil
1 large onion, finely chopped
2 large leeks, thinly sliced
2 large carrots, diced
1 small red pepper, seeded and diced
1¼ cups boiling water
2 tomatoes, peeled and chopped
⅓ cup seedless raisins
1 cup diced Cheddar cheese
salt and freshly ground black pepper

1 Melt half the butter with the oil in a large saucepan. Add the onion, leeks, carrots and red pepper, cover and cook gently about 20 minutes.

2 Meanwhile, melt the remaining butter in a large saucepan. Add the bulgur wheat and stir until the grains are thoroughly coated with butter. Stir in the boiling water, cover and place over gentle heat. Cook 10 minutes until the water has been absorbed.

3 Using a fork, gently mix the cooked vegetables into the bulgur wheat. Lightly stir in the tomatoes, raisins and cheese and fork through until the cheese is melted. Season to taste with salt and pepper. Transfer to a warmed serving dish and serve at once.

Cook's Notes

TIME
This is a quick dish to make: the preparation and cooking only take about 30 minutes.

DID YOU KNOW
Bulgur wheat is wheat which has been cracked by a steaming process. It is widely used in Middle Eastern cooking and can be bought from health food shops and specialty food stores. It is sometimes also known simply as "cracked wheat".

● 500 calories per portion

Cabbage gratin

SERVES 4

1 green cabbage, weighing approximately 1 lb, coarsely shredded
1 teaspoon salt
6 juniper berries, crushed (optional)
2 tablespoons butter
2 tablespoons all-purpose flour
⅔ cup milk
⅔ cup light cream
pinch of white pepper
pinch of cayenne pepper
½ teaspoon freshly grated nutmeg
3 tablespoons fresh bread crumbs
¼ cup grated Cheddar or Monterey Jack cheese
extra 1 tablespoon butter

1 Preheat the oven to 375°.
2 Cook the cabbage until just tender, but still crisp, in boiling salted water. Drain thoroughly and mix in the juniper berries, if used.
3 Make a thick creamy sauce with the butter, flour, milk and cream mixed (see Preparation). Add salt, peppers and nutmeg, then taste and adjust seasoning; the sauce should be very highly flavored.
4 Stir the cabbage into the sauce and pour into a buttered ovenproof dish.
5 Mix together the bread crumbs and grated cheese. Sprinkle over the cabbage and sauce and top with flecks of butter.
6 Cook about 15 minutes and then increase oven temperature to 425°. Cook a further 10 minutes, until the cheese has melted and the top is crisp and bubbling.

Cook's Notes

TIME
Preparation 20 minutes, cooking 20-25 minutes.

SERVING IDEAS
Add peeled, chopped tomatoes to the sauce and scatter some crispy, fried bacon bits on top to make a complete supper dish.
Serve as an accompaniment to broiled or roast meat.

PREPARATION
To make the sauce: Melt the butter in a small saucepan, sprinkle in the flour and stir over a low heat 1-2 minutes until straw-colored. Remove from the heat and gradually stir in the milk and cream. Return to the heat and simmer, stirring, until thick and smooth.

VARIATIONS
Substitute cauliflower for cabbage to make the classic dish, cauliflower cheese. If you like your vegetable gratin really cheesy, add ¼ cup more cheese to the sauce. Mixing a little mustard into the white sauce in Stage 3 makes it a bit more tangy (you will need about ¼-½ teaspoon).

● 225 calories per portion

Creamy rutabaga bake

SERVES 4

2 lb rutabaga, cut into 1½-inch
   pieces
3 tablespoons butter or margarine
salt and freshly ground black pepper
freshly grated nutmeg
1 bunch scallions, chopped
2 tablespoons light cream
3-4 tablespoons fresh white bread
   crumbs
vegetable oil, for greasing

1 Preheat the oven to 375°. Lightly grease an ovenproof dish or casserole.
2 Put rutabaga in a large saucepan with just enough cold water to cover. Bring to a boil, then lower the heat. Cover, simmer 20 minutes or until tender, then drain.
3 Mash the rutabaga with 2 tablespoons butter; season. Stir in nutmeg, scallions and cream.
4 Put rutabaga mixture into the greased dish, smooth the top and sprinkle evenly with the bread crumbs. Dot with the remaining butter. Bake 40 minutes, until golden on top. Serve hot.

Cook's Notes

TIME
Preparation takes about 30 minutes, cooking 40 minutes.

ECONOMY
Save fuel by serving the bake with a main course such as cottage pie, savory ground beef or a quiche which can be baked in the oven at the same time.

● 120 calories per portion

Stir-fried celery

SERVES 4

1 head celery, stalks cut into ½-inch
   diagonal slices
1-2 tablespoons vegetable oil
3 scallions, thinly sliced
salt and freshly ground black pepper
2 tablespoons slivered almonds
2 tablespoons dry sherry
1 teaspoon soy sauce
1 teaspoon tomato paste
½ teaspoon superfine sugar
¼ teaspoon ground ginger

1 Heat the oil in a large skillet. Add
the sliced celery and scallions and
season with salt and pepper. Stir-fry
over moderate heat 5-7 minutes,
until the celery has lost its raw taste
but is still crunchy (see Cook's tip).
Add the almonds and stir-fry 1
minute.
2 Mix together the remaining
ingredients, pour into the pan and
stir-fry 2 minutes. Serve at once.

Cook's Notes

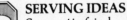

TIME
Preparation takes 15
minutes, cooking 10
minutes.

SERVING IDEAS
Serve stir-fried celery as
part of a Chinese meal
that you have prepared yourself
or bought from a takeaway. It
goes well with almost any meat
or fish dish, or with a savory flan
or a vegetarian dish such as
macaroni cheese.

VARIATIONS
If you do not have any
dry sherry, you can use
vermouth or white wine
instead.

COOK'S TIP
Use a wooden spoon or
spatula to stir-fry,
keeping the ingredients on the
move all the time, so that they
cook evenly.

● 85 calories per portion

Cheesy eggplant bake

SERVES 4

2 eggplants
salt
½ cup vegetable oil
6 oz Swiss or mozzarella cheese,
  very thinly sliced
  (see Economy)
1 egg
1 can (about 8 oz) tomatoes
½ onion, finely chopped
1 tablespoon tomato paste
1 tablespoon water
salt and freshly ground black pepper
butter for greasing
1 large tomato, sliced

1 Cut the eggplants into about ¼-inch slices and put them in a strainer in layers, sprinkling salt between each layer. Cover with a plate and place a heavy weight on top. Leave about 1 hour to draw out the bitter juices, then rinse the slices under cold running water and pat dry on paper towels.

2 Preheat the oven to 350°. Grease a shallow baking dish.

3 Pour enough of the oil into a large skillet to cover the base. Heat the oil, put a layer of eggplant slices in the pan and cook 3-4 minutes on each side, turning once, until golden brown on both sides. Remove from the pan and drain on paper towels. Continue in the same way until all the eggplant slices are browned.

4 Place layers of eggplant and cheese alternatively in prepared dish, finishing with a layer of cheese on top.

5 Put the egg, canned tomatoes, onion, tomato paste and water in a blender and blend until smooth. Season with a little salt and pepper, then pour over the eggplants and the cheese. Arrange the tomato slices on top.

6 Bake, uncovered 25 minutes, until heated through and bubbling. Serve straight from the dish.

Cook's Notes

TIME
Once the eggplants are drained, preparation will take about 30 minutes, baking the dish in the oven takes 25 minutes.

ECONOMY
While the Swiss or mozzarella cheese gives the best flavor to this dish, a less expensive sharp Cheddar cheese can be used as a substitute quite successfully.

SERVING IDEAS
Serve this dish with plenty of warm, fresh bread and a green salad as a vegetarian meal.

●405 calories per portion

Creamed lemon spinach

SERVES 4

1½ lb fresh spinach leaves
1 teaspoon salt
2 tablespoons butter
1 tablespoon all-purpose flour
⅔ cup heavy cream
grated rind and juice of ½ lemon
freshly ground black pepper
pinch of freshly grated nutmeg
2 hard-cooked eggs, yolks and
   whites separated and finely
   chopped, to garnish

1 If using fresh spinach, thoroughly wash it in several changes of cold water to remove all the grit. Remove the stems and midribs and discard. Put the spinach in a large saucepan with just the water that clings to the leaves after washing. [!] Sprinkle over the salt.

2 Cook the spinach over moderate heat about 15 minutes, stirring occasionally with a wooden spoon. Turn the cooked spinach into a strainer and drain thoroughly, pressing the spinach with a large spoon or a saucer to extract as much moisture as possible.

3 Melt the butter in the rinsed-out pan, sprinkle in the flour and stir over moderate heat 3 minutes. Remove from heat, pour in the cream, and when it is completely blended, add the lemon rind and juice. [!] Season to taste with salt, pepper and nutmeg. Stir the spinach into the cream sauce and return to very low heat, just to heat through. [!]

4 Turn the spinach into a heated serving dish and arrange the chopped hard-cooked eggs in rows over the top. Serve at once.

Cook's Notes

TIME
Preparation, if using fresh spinach, takes about 15 minutes. Cooking takes about 20 minutes.

WATCHPOINTS
It is best to cook spinach in its own juices – added water only makes it soggy.

Do not add lemon juice until butter, flour and cream are well blended. Otherwise, the acid will curdle the cream.

On no account allow the cream sauce to boil when heating through, or it will curdle.

BUYING GUIDE
If fresh spinach is not available, use 2 packages (10 oz each) frozen cut leaf spinach, thawed and all moisture pressed out. Stir into the sauce and cook 5 minutes.

● 295 calories per portion

Carrots in orange juice

3 Increase the heat and boil the carrots 4-5 minutes until the amount of cooking liquid has reduced to a few tablespoonfuls. [!]

4 Transfer the carrots to a warmed serving dish and pour over the remaining cooking liquid. Garnish in one corner with the twist of orange and the sprig of parsley. Serve at once.

SERVES 4
1½ lb small carrots, thinly sliced
finely grated rind of ½ orange
juice of 1 orange
2 tablespoons butter or
    margarine
1 teaspoon light brown sugar
½ teaspoon salt
freshly ground black pepper

TO GARNISH
twist of orange (see Preparation)
sprig of parsley

1 Put the sliced carrots in a saucepan with the orange rind and juice, butter, sugar, salt and pepper to taste. Add enough cold water to cover the carrots.
2 Bring to a boil over high heat, then simmer very gently, uncovered, over the lowest possible heat 40-45 minutes, until the carrots are just tender.

Cook's Notes

TIME
20 minutes preparation, then 45-50 minutes cooking.

VARIATION
Use the finely grated rind of 1 lemon and 2 tablespoons lemon juice in place of the orange rind and juice.

SERVING IDEAS
This dish makes a refreshing accompaniment to any chicken, beef or lamb dish.

WATCHPOINT
The carrots are boiled for the last 4-5 minutes of cooking to evaporate the water and give the remaining cooking liquid a more concentrated flavor. This is known in cookery terms as "reduction". Be careful that you do not reduce the liquid too far, or the little that remains will burn on the base of the pan.

PREPARATION
To make a twist of orange to garnish the carrots, cut a thin slice from the halved orange before you grate it. Cut through the orange slice to the center, then twist each half in opposite directions. Keep covered with plastic wrap until required.

● 100 calories per portion

Peperonata

SERVES 4

4 red or green peppers, seeded and
    cut into thin strips
2 tablespoons butter
2 tablespoons vegetable oil
1 onion, chopped
8 large tomatoes, peeled and
    chopped (see Preparation)
1 clove garlic, crushed
pinch of sugar
salt and freshly ground black pepper

1 Heat the butter in a saucepan with
the oil. Add the peppers and onion
and cook gently 5 minutes until the
onion is soft and lightly colored.
Cover the pan with a lid and
continue frying gently until the
peppers are soft.

2 Add the tomatoes, garlic, sugar
and salt and pepper to taste. Stir
gently.
3 Cover and simmer over a very
low heat, stirring from time to time,
25-30 minutes, or until the mixture
is soft and the tomato juices have
evaporated.
4 Spoon the mixture into a warmed
serving dish and either serve hot or
allow to cool and serve cold, but not
chilled.

Cook's Notes

TIME
Easy to make, this dish
takes 20 minutes to
prepare and 25-30 minutes to
cook.

PREPARATION
It is important to peel
the tomatoes: put them
in a bowl, cover with boiling
water and leave 1 minute.
Remove with a slotted spoon,
plunge into a bowl of cold
water, then peel off the skins
with a sharp knife.

SERVING IDEAS
This versatile casserole
of peppers and to-
matoes can be served hot with
broiled meat or fish, or cold as a
side salad or starter.

DID YOU KNOW
This dish originates
from Italy, where
peppers and tomatoes grow in
abundance. An Italian cook
would use olive oil for frying.

● 150 calories per portion

Peas portugaise

SERVES 4

3 cups frozen peas
2 tablespoons vegetable oil
1 medium onion, finely chopped
1 clove garlic, crushed (optional)
2 teaspoons paprika
1 can (about 14 oz) tomatoes (see Variation)
1 teaspoon superfine sugar
celery salt and freshly ground black pepper

1 Heat the oil in a saucepan, add the onion and garlic, if using, and cook over moderate heat 3-4 minutes, stirring occasionally, until the onion is soft but not colored. Stir in the paprika and cook a further 2 minutes, then stir in the tomatoes with their juice, the sugar, celery salt and pepper to taste. Bring to a boil, lower the heat and simmer, uncovered, for about 10 minutes or until the tomato sauce is reduced to a thick purée. ✳

2 Meanwhile, cook the peas in a small quantity of boiling salted water, according to package directions. Drain well.

3 Turn the peas into a warmed serving dish. Taste and adjust the seasoning of the tomato sauce, then spoon it over the peas and fork through lightly so that the sauce can run through the peas to flavor them. Serve the peas at once, while very hot.

Cook's Notes

TIME
Total preparation and cooking time is 15-20 minutes.

COOK'S TIP
The tomato sauce can be made separately and used with other vegetables.

SERVING IDEAS
The dish may be garnished with small points of toasted or fried bread.

VARIATION
When tomatoes are cheap and plentiful, use 1 lb fresh tomatoes instead of canned.

FREEZING
The tomato sauce can be frozen in a rigid container or plastic bag for up to 2 months. To serve: Reheat from frozen in a heavy-based saucepan, stirring frequently.

● 145 calories per portion

Baked potatoes with apple

SERVES 4

4 large potatoes, about ½ lb each
(see Buying guide)
½ medium green apple
2 tablespoons butter or margarine
1 large onion, finely chopped
4 sage leaves, chopped, or 1
teaspoon dried sage
½ teaspoon dry mustard
salt
butter, for greasing

Cook's Notes

TIME
Preparation 15 minutes, cooking, including baking potatoes, 1¾ hours.

SERVING IDEAS
These potatoes are especially good served with pork or ham.

For a snack meal, top each potato with ¼ cup of grated Cheddar cheese and broil under moderate heat until the cheese is golden brown.

BUYING GUIDE
Idaho or russet potatoes are best for baking.

CHILDREN
The apple-baked potatoes would make a nutritious light meal for children. As young children might find the flavor of sage and mustard too strong, it would be advisable to omit these ingredients.

● 280 calories per portion

---

1 Preheat the oven to 400°.

2 Scrub the potatoes and with a fork prick each one in 2 places on both sides. Bake the potatoes in the oven 1½ hours.

3 Remove the potatoes from the oven (leaving the oven on), allow to cool slightly, then cut each one in half lengthwise. Scoop the cooked potato into a bowl, leaving the shells intact. Mash the potato well.

Pare, core and finely chop the apple.
4 Melt the butter in a small skillet add the onion and cook gently until it begins to soften, stirring occasionally. Stir in the apple and cook a further 2-3 minutes, until soft.

5 Stir the apple and onion mixture into the mashed potato. Add the sage, mustard and a little salt. Mix thoroughly.

6 Spoon the mixture back into the potato shells and make criss-cross patterns on the top with a fork for a decorative finish.

7 Put the potato shells in a greased shallow ovenproof dish and return to the oven. Bake 15 minutes until the tops are browned. Serve piping hot. Alternatively, top the potatoes with grated cheese (see Serving ideas).

Cabbage and lemon sauce

SERVES 4-6

1 large green cabbage, finely sliced
salt

SAUCE
4 teaspoons butter or margarine
1½ tablespoons all-purpose
** flour**
1¼ cups warm milk
grated rind and juice of 1 large
** lemon**
freshly grated nutmeg
freshly ground black pepper
lemon slices and 2 teaspoons chives,
** to garnish (see Variations)**

1 Bring a saucepan of salted water to a boil.
2 Meanwhile, make the sauce: Melt the butter in a separate saucepan, sprinkle in the flour and stir over a low heat 1-2 minutes until straw-colored. Remove from the heat and gradually stir in the milk. Return to heat; or simmer, stirring, until thickened and smooth.
3 Plunge the cabbage into the boiling water and boil gently 5 minutes, stirring frequently.
4 Stir the lemon rind and juice into the sauce, then season to taste with nutmeg, and plenty of salt and pepper (see Cook's tip).
5 Drain the cabbage well, then return to the rinsed-out pan. Pour in the sauce, then toss over gentle heat until the cabbage is lightly coated in the sauce. [!]
6 Turn into a warmed serving dish. Garnish with the lemon slices and chives and serve at once.

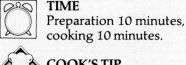

Cook's Notes

TIME
Preparation 10 minutes, cooking 10 minutes.

COOK'S TIP
The sauce needs plenty of salt to bring out the lemon flavor.

WATCHPOINT
It is essential that the cabbage is tossed quickly in the sauce, so that it still has a "bite" to it. Do not overcook it at this stage, or the finished dish will be soggy.

VARIATIONS
If chives are not available, use finely chopped scallion tops instead. Or use fresh tarragon if available.

SERVING IDEAS
The lemon sauce makes this a delicious accompaniment to poached, broiled or fried white fish.
It is also good with a joint of roast lamb or broiled lamb chops or cutlets.

● 125 calories per portion

Snow peas with water chestnuts

SERVES 4

½ lb snow peas (see Buying guide)
2 tablespoons vegetable oil
4 scallions, cut into 2-inch lengths
1 can (about 8 oz) water chestnuts, drained and sliced
2 tablespoons soy sauce
½ teaspoon sugar
4 tablespoons chicken broth
salt and freshly ground black pepper

1 Top and tail the snow peas and, if necessary, remove any strings from the pod sides.
2 Heat the oil in a wok or a large skillet, add the scallions, snow peas and water chestnuts and stir until the vegetables are coated with oil.
3 Add the soy sauce, sugar and chicken broth and stir-fry over moderate heat about 5 minutes, stirring constantly, until the vegetables are hot but still crisp.
4 Season to taste with salt and pepper, turn into a warmed serving dish and serve at once.

Cook's Notes

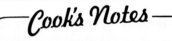

TIME
15 minutes preparation and cooking.

SERVING IDEAS
Serve as part of a Chinese meal with a beef dish or crispy roast duck.

BUYING GUIDE
Snow peas tend to be quite expensive, but are well worth buying occasionally for their delicate flavor.
   If fresh snow peas are not available, buy them frozen from freezer centers.

VARIATION
Use about 1 cup sliced mushrooms instead of the water chestnuts.

● 100 calories per portion

Brussels sprouts country style

SERVES 4

1½ lb Brussels sprouts
salt

1 tablespoon vegetable oil
1 large onion, sliced
1 green pepper, seeded and chopped
1 lb tomatoes
½ teaspoon dried basil
freshly ground black pepper

1 Trim the sprouts. Wash them thoroughly and cut a cross in the base of each one.
2 Cook the sprouts in boiling salted water until just tender (about 10-12 minutes). [!] Drain well.
3 Meanwhile, heat the oil in a skillet over moderate heat. Fry the onion and green pepper until the pepper is soft and the onion brown.
4 Peel the tomatoes and chop them roughly (see Preparation).
5 Add the sprouts, tomatoes and basil to the pan and heat through. Season well with black pepper and serve immediately.

Cook's Notes

TIME
Preparation of vegetables will take 20 minutes. Cook Brussels sprouts and soften onion and peppers 10-15 minutes. Heat through about 10 minutes.

WATCHPOINT
Never overcook sprouts or they will color and become soggy.

SERVING IDEAS
Serve with any savory dish, from an omelet to a roast.
To turn Brussels sprouts country style into a supper dish, add slices of bacon to the onion and pepper mixture.

SPECIAL OCCASION
Add ½ cup dairy sour cream to the Brussels sprouts country-style. Stir in well before serving.

● 95 calories per portion

PREPARATION
Tomatoes can be peeled easily as shown below.

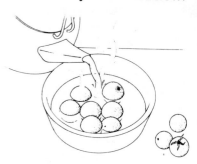

1 Cover the tomatoes with boiling water and leave 1 minute, then plunge into cold water.

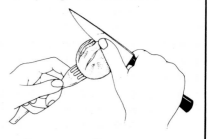

2 Remove with a fork and use a sharp knife to take away the skin which will peel off easily.

Creamed onions

SERVES 4-6

1½ lb onions
salt
⅔ cup dairy sour cream
freshly ground black pepper
paprika
2 tablespoons butter or margarine
4 tablespoons day-old white bread
    crumbs (see Cook's tip)
1 tablespoon chopped fresh parsley
2 hard-cooked eggs
parsley, to garnish

 TIME
Preparation takes 30-40 minutes, cooking in the oven 15 minutes.

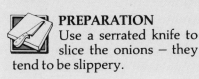 **COOK'S TIP**
Use day-old, not absolutely fresh, bread crumbs to ensure that they cook crisply.

PREPARATION
Use a serrated knife to slice the onions — they tend to be slippery.

WATCHPOINT
Watch the bread crumbs carefully, since they brown very easily.

SERVING IDEAS
Serve with lamb, instead of onion sauce.

ECONOMY
For a slightly less expensive version, use white sauce instead of cream.

● 215 calories per portion

---

1 Cook the onions in boiling salted water 15-20 minutes. Drain them thoroughly, reserving 1 tablespoon of the cooking liquid. Leave the onions to cool slightly, then pat them dry with paper towels.

2 Preheat the oven to 350°.

3 Put the onions on a board and slice them (see Preparation). Arrange the sliced onions in an ovenproof dish.

4 Beat dairy sour cream with the reserved onion liquid and season with salt, pepper and paprika to taste. Pour the cream over the onions in the dish.

5 Melt the butter in a small skillet, add the bread crumbs and cook about 5 minutes over moderate heat, stirring frequently, until they are golden and crisp. [!]

6 Remove the pan from the heat and stir in the parsley. Chop 1 hard-cooked egg and stir it into the fried crumb mixture. Spoon the mixture evenly over the onions.

7 Bake in the oven 15 minutes. Meanwhile, slice the remaining hard-cooked egg.

8 Arrange the egg slices in a row along the top of the dish. Sprinkle with paprika, garnish with parsley and serve at once.

Farmhouse lentils

SERVES 4

1 cup split red lentils
1 tablespoon vegetable oil
1 large onion, thinly sliced
3¾ cups chicken broth
1 lb potatoes, cut into even-sized
  chunks
4 tomatoes, peeled, quartered and
  seeded
½ teaspoon dried marjoram or
  thyme
½ teaspoon paprika
salt and freshly ground black
  pepper
¾ cup frozen peas
1 cup thinly sliced small mushrooms

1 Heat the oil in a large saucepan, add the onion and cook over moderate heat about 3-4 minutes, stirring occasionally.
2 Add the broth to the pan and bring to a boil. Add the lentils, potatoes, tomatoes, herbs, paprika and salt and pepper to taste. Stir well then cover and simmer 20 minutes, stirring occasionally.
3 Add the frozen peas and mushrooms to the pan, cover and simmer a further 5-10 minutes, stirring occasionally, until the lentils are soft and the potatoes are cooked.
4 To serve: Taste and adjust seasoning, then transfer to a warmed shallow dish. Serve hot.

Cook's Notes

TIME
Preparation 10 minutes, cooking 30-45 minutes.

WATCHPOINT
It is important to stir the simmering mixture from time to time, to prevent it sticking to the base of the pan as it cooks.

SERVING IDEAS
This dish would go very well with bacon or ham, or plump sausages — especially herb-flavored ones.

● 355 calories per portion

Green beans provençal

SERVES 4

1 package (about ¾ lb) frozen green
   beans
1 tablespoon vegetable oil
1 medium onion, chopped
1 large clove garlic, crushed
½ lb tomatoes, peeled and chopped
1 teaspoon dried basil
salt and freshly ground black
   pepper

1 Heat the oil in a heavy-based
saucepan. Add the onion and garlic
and cook gently 10-15 minutes, or
until the onion is soft.
2 Add the tomatoes, plus the basil

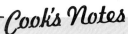
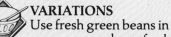

and salt and pepper to taste, then
simmer over moderate heat,
uncovered, 10 minutes, stirring
occasionally.
3 Meanwhile, cook the beans
according to package directions in
boiling salted water until they are
tender but still crisp to the bite.
Drain thoroughly.
4 Stir the beans into the tomato
mixture, then taste and adjust
seasoning. Serve hot.

New potatoes with wine

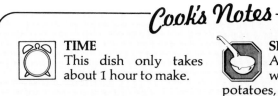

SERVES 4

1½ lb new potatoes, scrubbed
2 tablespoons butter
½ small can anchovies, drained, soaked in milk for 20 minutes, then drained and chopped
1 tablespoon finely chopped fresh mint, chives or parsley
salt and freshly ground black pepper
⅔ cup dry white wine
1 tablespoon finely grated Parmesan cheese

1 Preheat the oven to 375° and grease a shallow ovenproof dish with half of the butter.
2 Bring the potatoes to a boil in salted water, lower the heat and cook 12-15 minutes or until barely tender. Drain and leave until cool enough to handle.
3 Slice the potatoes into the prepared dish, sprinkling each layer with anchovies, mint, chives or parsley and salt and pepper to taste. !
4 Pour the wine over the top, then sprinkle evenly with Parmesan cheese and then finally dot the potatoes with the remaining butter.
5 Bake above center of the oven for about 30 minutes or until the potatoes are cooked through and the top is crisp and golden brown. Serve at once, straight from the dish (see Serving ideas).

Cook's Notes

TIME
This dish only takes about 1 hour to make.

ECONOMY
Cook the potatoes in this style when the oven is already in use for other dishes, for example, when roasting meat or poultry (see Serving ideas) or baking.

WATCHPOINT
Anchovies are salty, so only a very light seasoning of salt is necessary.

SERVING IDEAS
A deliciously different way of cooking new potatoes, this dish can be served as a light meal with crisply broiled bacon or topped with poached eggs, or as an unusual and tasty vegetable accompaniment to roast meat and poultry.

Because this dish includes anchovies, it is also particularly suitable for serving with a main course of fish.

● 220 calories per portion

SPICY VEGETABLES

Curried cauliflower salad

SERVES 4

1 medium cauliflower, broken into bite-sized flowerets
2 medium dessert apples
2 medium carrots, coarsely grated
½ cup golden raisins

DRESSING

1 tablespoon vegetable oil
10 scallions, trimmed and finely chopped
2 teaspoons hot curry powder
6 tablespoons mayonnaise
1 tablespoon lemon juice
salt and freshly ground black pepper

1 To make the dressing: Heat the oil in a skillet, add scallions and cook over gentle heat until they begin to brown. Stir in the curry powder and cook 1-2 minutes, then remove from the heat and leave to cool slightly. Stir in the mayonnaise and lemon juice, then season to taste with salt and pepper.

2 Plunge the cauliflower into a saucepan of boiling salted water, then blanch by boiling 2 minutes (see Cook's tip). Drain and immediately refresh under cold running water. Drain the cauliflower flowerets thoroughly again, then put them into a large bowl.

3 Core and dice the apples, but do not pare them. Add to the cauliflower with the carrots and raisins, then fold gently to mix, being careful not to break up the cauliflower. Add the dressing and gently toss the vegetables in it, turning them over lightly with a fork, to coat them evenly.

4 Pile the salad into a serving bowl. Cover tightly with plastic wrap and chill the salad in the refrigerator for at least 2 hours. Remove the salad from the refrigerator 10 minutes before serving.

Cook's Notes

TIME
Preparation, including making the dressing, takes 30 minutes. Allow at least 2 hours for chilling the salad.

SERVING IDEAS
This is a versatile salad which can be served with any cold meal, or as part of a buffet. It would make a tasty part of an hors d'oeuvre selection, or it could be served on its own as an appetizer.

VARIATION
Use 1 medium onion, finely chopped, if scallions are not available.

COOK'S TIP
Blanching the cauliflower slightly lessens its strong flavor, and flowerets remain quite crisp. However, if you want a very crunchy salad, use the cauliflower raw.

● 280 calories per portion

Spicy potato sticks

SERVES

1 lb even-sized potatoes
salt
2 cloves garlic, crushed
1 small onion, finely chopped
1 teaspoon ground cumin
1 teaspoon ground turmeric
½ teaspoon chili powder
2 tablespoons water
vegetable oil, for frying

1 Boil the potatoes in salted water 5 minutes. Drain in a strainer then rinse under cold running water until cool enough to handle. Pat dry on paper towels.

2 Cut the potatoes into ¼-inch thick slices, then cut each slice lengthwise into ⅛-inch wide sticks. Set aside.

3 Put the garlic with the onion, spices, 1 teaspoon salt and the water into a blender and blend until the mixture is very smooth.

4 Heat 1 tablespoon oil in a large skillet add the spice mixture and cook gently 5 minutes, stirring often. Remove from heat.

5 Fill a large heavy-based skillet to a depth of ½-inch with oil and heat until stale bread cube browns in 50 seconds.

6 Cook a batch of the potato sticks in the oil until golden. [!] Remove with a slotted spoon and drain on paper towels. Cook the rest.

7 While cooking the last batch, return the pan of spice mixture to low heat and heat through.

8 Add the potato sticks to the spice mixture and toss to coat well.

9 Turn the sticks into a warmed serving dish and serve at once.

Cook's Notes

TIME
Preparation and cooking take about 20 minutes in total.

COOK'S TIP
This is a mildly spicy dish – for a hotter taste, increase the amount of chili powder slightly.

SERVING IDEAS
These tasty potato sticks are excellent for brightening up plain dishes such as roast or broiled chicken or lamb. Alternatively, they make a delicious addition to an Indian meal.

For a dash of color, garnish with fresh coriander sprigs.

WATCHPOINT
During cooking, move the potato sticks occasionally with a spatula to prevent them from sticking, but be very gentle or they will break up. There is no need to turn the sticks in this depth of oil.

● 195 calories per portion

Indonesian salads

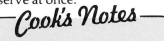

SERVES 4

¼ lb beansprouts
1 can (about 8 oz) pineapple rings
   (see Buying guide)
3-inch length of cucumber,
   diced
1 dessert apple
juice of ½ lemon

SAUCE
2 tablespoons smooth peanut butter
2 teaspoons soy sauce
juice of ½ lemon

1 Divide the beansprouts between 4 serving plates.
2 Drain the pineapple, reserving the juice, and chop finely. Put in a bowl and set aside.
3 Make the sauce: Put the peanut butter in a bowl and beat in the soy sauce and lemon juice to form a thick cream. Add about 2 tablespoons of the reserved pineapple juice. Set aside.
4 Mix the cucumber into the chopped pineapple. Core and dice the apple, toss in the lemon juice and add to the pineapple mixture. Immediately divide this mixture between the 4 plates, piling it onto the beansprouts.
5 Pour the sauce over each salad and serve at once.

Cook's Notes

TIME
This quickly prepared dish only takes about 15 minutes to make.

BUYING GUIDE
If you are watching your weight, look out for pineapple rings in natural fruit juice. These do not have any added sugar and so the calorie count will be lower.

SERVING IDEAS
Serve this tasty and refreshing salad as a appetizer or as an accompaniment.

● 85 calories per portion

Okra Mediterranean-style

SERVES 4

1 lb okra (see Buying guide and
    Preparation)
4 tablespoons vegetable oil
1 large onion, chopped
1 lb tomatoes, peeled and quartered
1 clove garlic, crushed
1 teaspoon ground coriander
salt and freshly ground black
    pepper
coriander leaves, to garnish

1 Heat the oil in a large saucepan,
add onion and cook 5 minutes.
2 Add the okra to the pan, stir to
coat well with the oil, then add the
tomatoes, garlic and coriander. Stir
well to mix, then season to taste.
3 Bring to a boil, then lower the
heat slightly, cover and simmer 30
minutes until okra is tender. Serve
garnished with coriander.

Cook's Notes

TIME
Preparation and cook-
ing take about 40 min-
utes in total.

SERVING IDEAS
This dish is a natural accompaniment to broiled
lamb chops or kabobs. It is also
delicious served with either
plain boiled or fried rice as a
main course.

BUYING GUIDE
Okra can be bought at
Asian, Greek and West
Indian food shops, as well as
specialty food stores and large
supermarkets.
    Canned okra is also available
and may be used in this recipe,
but the flavor and texture will
not be as good.

● 165 calories per portion

PREPARATION
To prepare the okra for
this dish:

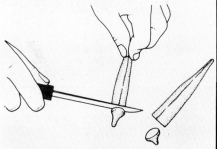

*Cut ends off the okra and remove
any blemishes with a sharp knife. It
is not necessary to pare the okra
before they are cooked.*

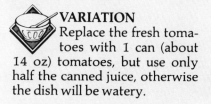
VARIATION
Replace the fresh toma-
toes with 1 can (about
14 oz) tomatoes, but use only
half the canned juice, otherwise
the dish will be watery.

Noodles Chinese-style

SERVES 4

¼ lb Chinese egg noodles (see Buying guide)

salt

2 tablespoons vegetable oil

6 scallions, sliced

1 tablespoon grated fresh root ginger

1 lb Chinese cabbage, cut into ½-inch thick slices

½ cup chopped lean cooked ham (see Economy)

¼ lb beansprouts

1 tablespoon soy sauce (see Buying guide)

4 tablespoons chicken broth, dry sherry or water

freshly ground black pepper

1 Bring a large saucepan of salted water to a boil. Add the noodles bring back to a boil and cook about 3 minutes or according to package directions, until just tender. Drain and set aside.

 TIME
10 minutes preparation, 10 minutes cooking.

ECONOMY
Any left-over lean cooked meat can be substituted for the ham.

SERVING IDEAS
This Chinese-style dish is particularly good served as a vegetable accompaniment to broiled or fried fish, chops or chicken.

To serve as a quick, economical light lunch or supper dish, double the quantities. If liked, add extra ingredients such as sliced mushrooms or cooked peeled shrimp.

 BUYING GUIDE
Thin Chinese egg noodles are available at supermarkets and specialty stores, but if difficult to obtain, Italian spaghetti or egg noodles can be used instead. These will need longer initial cooking in water — follow package directions.

Some supermarkets may have a choice of soy sauces — choose the lighter type for this dish.

● 230 calories per portion

2 Heat the oil in a wok or large skillet add the scallions and ginger and cook gently 2 minutes, stirring constantly.

3 Add the Chinese cabbage to pan with the chopped ham. Cook a further 2 minutes, stirring the mixture constantly.

4 Add the drained noodles, together with the beansprouts, soy sauce, broth and salt and pepper to taste. Increase the heat to moderate and stir-fry about 5 minutes until the vegetables are tender but still crisp and most of the liquid in the pan has evaporated.

5 Taste and adjust seasoning. Turn into a warmed serving dish.

Stir-fried beans and beansprouts

SERVES 4

½ lb small French beans, left whole
  (see Buying guide)
2 tablespoons vegetable oil
1 onion, sliced
4 tablespoons water
1 tablespoon light soy sauce
1 tablespoon lemon juice
salt and freshly ground black pepper
½ cup sliced mushrooms (see
  Buying guide)
½ lb beansprouts

1 Heat the oil in a wok or large heavy-based pan. Cook the onion 2 minutes, then add the beans and stir-fry 1 minute.

2 Add the water, soy sauce, lemon juice and season to taste with salt and pepper. Cook 5 minutes, tossing the beans in the liquid until it has evaporated.

3 Add the mushrooms and stir constantly until they are tender. Add beansprouts and stir-fry a further 2 minutes until the beansprouts are heated through and just tender, but still crisp. Transfer to a warmed serving dish and serve at once (see Serving ideas).

Cook's Notes

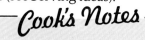
TIME
Preparation time is 5 minutes and cooking time about 10 minutes.

SERVING IDEAS
This crunchy dish makes an excellent accompaniment to roast or broiled meats, particularly steaks and chops.

BUYING GUIDE
Small, thin French beans are best for stir-frying and they will give the crunchiest result.
Choose small mushrooms for this recipe — they make an attractive addition and will give the dish a lighter color.

● 85 calories per portion

Chinese lettuce parcels

SERVES 6

6 large crisp lettuce leaves (see Preparation)
2 tablespoons vegetable oil
4 scallions, finely chopped
1 teaspoon ground ginger
1 celery stalk, finely chopped
¾ cup finely chopped mushrooms
2 oz canned water chestnuts, drained and finely sliced
1 cup cooked long-grain rice
¾ cup frozen peas, cooked and drained
1½ tablespoons soy sauce
1 egg, beaten
extra soy sauce, to serve

1 Heat the oil in a wok or large skillet. Add the scallions and ginger and cook gently 2-3 minutes until soft.

2 Add the celery, mushrooms and water chestnuts and cook a further 5 minutes.

3 Stir in the rice, peas and soy sauce. Remove the pan from the heat and stir in the egg.

4 Lay the lettuce leaves out flat on a work surface. Put about 2 generous tablespoons of the mixture at the base of each lettuce leaf. Fold the leaf around the mixture and roll up to form neat parcels. Secure with toothpicks, if necessary.

5 Place the parcels in a steamer. If you do not have a steamer, use a metal strainer which fits neatly inside a saucepan (the base must not touch the water). Fill the pan with boiling water, place the parcels in the strainer and place the strainer in the pan. Cover with foil or lid of steamer and steam 5 minutes.

6 Remove the toothpicks from the parcels, if using, then place the parcels on a warmed serving dish. Serve at once, with extra soy sauce handed separately.

Cauliflower creole

SERVES 4

1 cauliflower
1 tablespoon vegetable oil
1 large onion, chopped
1 clove garlic, crushed (optional)
1 can (about 14 oz) tomatoes
salt
2 tablespoons butter or margarine
1 large green pepper, seeded and
  chopped
½–1 teaspoon hot-pepper sauce
freshly ground black pepper

1 Heat the oil in a large saucepan, add the onion and garlic, if using, and cook 2-3 minutes until just tender.
2 Stir in the tomatoes, breaking them up against the sides of the pan with a wooden spoon. Cover and simmer gently 20-30 minutes.
3 Meanwhile, bring a pan of salted water to boil, plunge the cauliflower head down in it and cook about 20 minutes [!] until just tender. Preheat the oven to 250°. Drain the cauliflower well, place on a warmed serving dish and keep hot in the oven.
4 Add the butter and green pepper to the tomato sauce, stir well and simmer 5 minutes. Season to taste with hot-pepper sauce and salt and pepper.
5 Pour a little of the sauce over the cauliflower, leaving some of the white flower showing. Pour the remaining sauce round the sides.

Sweet and sour Brussels sprouts

SERVES 4

1¼ lb fresh Brussels sprouts (see Buying guide), or 1 package (1 lb) frozen sprouts
¼ cup butter or margarine
1 medium onion, finely chopped
2 dessert apples
2 tablespoons seedless raisins
3 tablespoons lemon juice (see Cook's tip)
3 tablespoons clear honey
salt and freshly ground black pepper

1 Cook the sprouts in boiling salted water about 10-15 minutes until just tender. If using frozen sprouts cook according to package directions.
2 Meanwhile, melt the butter in a saucepan, add the onion and cook gently until soft but not colored. Pare, core and chop the apples fairly coarsely, then add to the onion with the raisins and stir well. Season well with salt and pepper.
3 Mix together the lemon juice and honey and pour into a pitcher.
4 When the sprouts are cooked, drain well, add to onion mixture and stir well to mix. Transfer to a serving bowl, pour over the sauce and serve.

Cook's Notes

TIME
Total preparation and cooking time, if using fresh sprouts, is 25 minutes.

VARIATIONS
Broccoli may be substituted for Brussels sprouts and any crisp dessert apple such as a Granny Smith, Jonathan or Red Delicious may be used.

COOK'S TIP
The average lemon yields 2 tablespoons of juice, so for this recipe you will need 1½ lemons.

BUYING GUIDE
When buying Brussels sprouts, choose ones which are small, compact and a good green color with no signs of yellowing. If buying sprouts packed in a package from a supermarket, make sure there are no signs of mold on them.

SERVING IDEAS
You can serve this unusual dish of Brussels sprouts in place of ordinary boiled sprouts with roast or broiled meats.

● 190 calories per portion

Oriental vegetable fritters

SERVES 4

1 large cauliflower, broken into bite-sized flowerets

2 bunches large scallions, trimmed and halved lengthwise

1 lb carrots, halved lengthwise and cut into 2½-inch lengths

vegetable oil, for deep-frying

BATTER

1 cup all-purpose flour

¼ teaspoon baking soda

¼ teaspoon salt

¼ teaspoon ground ginger

1 egg yolk

¾ cup cold water

DIPPING SAUCE

3 tablespoons tomato paste

1½ tablespoons soy sauce

1½ tablespoons clear honey

4 tablespoons chicken broth

1 Make the dipping sauce: Stir together the ingredients for the sauce, then divide the mixture between 4 custard cups or small dishes. Set aside.

2 Make the batter: Sift the flour, baking soda, salt and ginger into a bowl. Beat the egg yolk with the cold water and gradually add to the flour, stirring with a wooden spoon, to make a smooth thin batter.

3 Preheat the oven to 250°. Heat the oil in a deep-fat frier to 375° or until a cube of bread browns in about 50 seconds.

4 Dip the vegetable pieces a few at a time into the batter. Transfer them to the hot oil with a slotted spoon and deep-fry for about 3 minutes or until golden brown, turning once with the spoon. Remove from the pan with the slotted spoon and drain well on paper towels. ☐ Arrange on a warmed large serving platter and keep warm in the oven while frying the remaining vegetables pieces in the same way.

5 Serve the fritters as soon as they are all cooked: Provide each person with a bowl of sauce so that they can dip their vegetables into it.

Cook's Notes

TIME
10-15 minutes preparation, then 30-40 minutes cooking.

WATCHPOINT
Use plenty of paper towels to drain the fritters, so that they are not excessively oily.

VARIATIONS
Delicious alternatives are thickly sliced zucchini, wide strips of green and red pepper, eggplant slices, whole small mushrooms and whole or halved French beans.

DID YOU KNOW
These fritters are a version of the Japanese tempura — vegetables deep fried in a batter. Tempura batter is different from other fritter batters because it contains no oil or butter and must be used immediately.

● 400 calories per portion

Vegetable biriani

SERVES 4-6

2 tablespoons vegetable oil
1 large onion, chopped
2 cloves garlic, crushed (optional)
2 teaspoons hot curry powder
½ teaspoon ground cinnamon
½ teaspoon ground ginger
2 cups water
1 tablespoon tomato paste
1 large carrot, diced
2 teaspoons salt
1 cup long-grain rice
½ cup seedless raisins
½ lb sliced runner or French beans,
   fresh or frozen
1 cup frozen peas

1 Heat the oil in a large saucepan. Add the onion and garlic, if using, and cook gently about 10 minutes until the onion is soft but not browned, stirring frequently.

Cook's Notes

TIME
Preparation and cooking take about 45 minutes.

WATCHPOINT
Try not to lift the lid of the pan during the cooking and do not stir unless absolutely necessary: this way the rice will be tender and fluffy. Heat must be low at this stage.

COOK'S TIP
If using frozen beans, cook them straight from the freezer, without thawing.

DID YOU KNOW
Biriani is an Indian rice dish usually served as an accompaniment to a main-course curry, although sometimes it has meat, fish or poultry added to it and is served with a curry sauce, in which case it becomes a main course in its own right. If you like the flavor of curry, you can serve this biriani as a vegetable accompaniment to any main-course meat or fish dish.

● 365 calories per portion

2 Add the spices to the pan, stir well and cook a further 2 minutes.
3 Add the water, tomato paste, carrot and salt. Bring to a boil.
4 Add the rice, raisins and fresh or frozen beans, and stir well (see Cook's tip).
5 Lower the heat, cover the pan tightly and simmer very gently 20 minutes, without stirring. ⚠
6 Gently fork in the frozen peas, cover the pan and simmer very gently a further 5 minutes. Taste and adjust seasoning. Pile the biriani into a warmed serving dish and serve hot.

Sambols

SERVES 5-6

½ lb tomatoes, peeled and
   chopped
2 tablespoons coconut milk, water
   and desiccated coconut
1 green chili, seeded and sliced
1 large onion, sliced
juice of ½ lemon (see Cook's tip)
salt
½ cucumber, thinly sliced
⅔ cup shredded coconut
2 tablespoons hot water
pinch of chili powder

1 Make the tomato sambol: Put the
tomatoes into a bowl and stir in half
the coconut milk, half the chili and
one-third of the onion. Mix well,
then add ½ teaspoon lemon juice
and season to taste with salt.

Cook's Notes

TIME
Tomato sambol: takes
15 minutes to prepare.
Cucumber sambol: Preparation
takes about 10 minutes plus 30
minutes salting. *Coconut sambol:*
takes 25 minutes including
standing time.

COOK'S TIP
Half a lemon should
yield at least 1 table-
spoon of juice.

DID YOU KNOW
Sambols are traditional
accompaniments to all
types of curry – serve 1 or all
of them. They are often served
in small dishes. For serving 10-
12 people, double the quantities
of ingredients that are used
here.

● 10 calories per tomato
● 10 calories per cucumber
● 30 calories per coconut

2 Make the cucumber sambol:
Arrange the cucumber slices in a
shallow dish and sprinkle with salt.
Leave for 30 minutes.
3 Meanwhile, make the coconut
sambol: Put coconut in bowl,
pour over hot water and leave 15
minutes. Stir in chili powder, one
third of onion and ½ teaspoon

lemon juice. Season with salt.
4 Rinse and pat the cucumber dry
and transfer to a bowl. Mix in the
remaining coconut milk, lemon
juice and almost all remaining green
chili and onion. Season with salt.
5 Transfer sambols to individual
dishes; garnish with onion and chili
rings and more chili powder.

INDEX

Picture credits
Bryce Atwell: 63
Martin Brigdale: 4, 42, 44, 76
Paul Bussell: 51, 69, 80
Alan Duns: 15, 30, 36, 58
Paul Forrester: 10, 40
Edmund Goldspink: 27, 49
James Jackson: 5, 7, 9, 11, 13, 18, 22,
    29, 43, 52, 53, 54, 57, 71
Michael Kay: 61
Paul Kemp: 37, 39, 48, 66
Chris Knaggs: 12, 24, 67, 73
Bob Komar: 6, 34
Don Last: 23, 33, 41, 70, 77, 78
David Levin: 38
Fred Mancini: 8, 25, 31, 46, 50, 56, 59,
    72
Peter Mayers: 14, 35, 45, 47, 55, 65
Roger Phillips: 21, 62, 74
Paul Webster: 17, 19, 20, 26, 60, 64
Paul Williams: 28
Graham Young: 68, 79